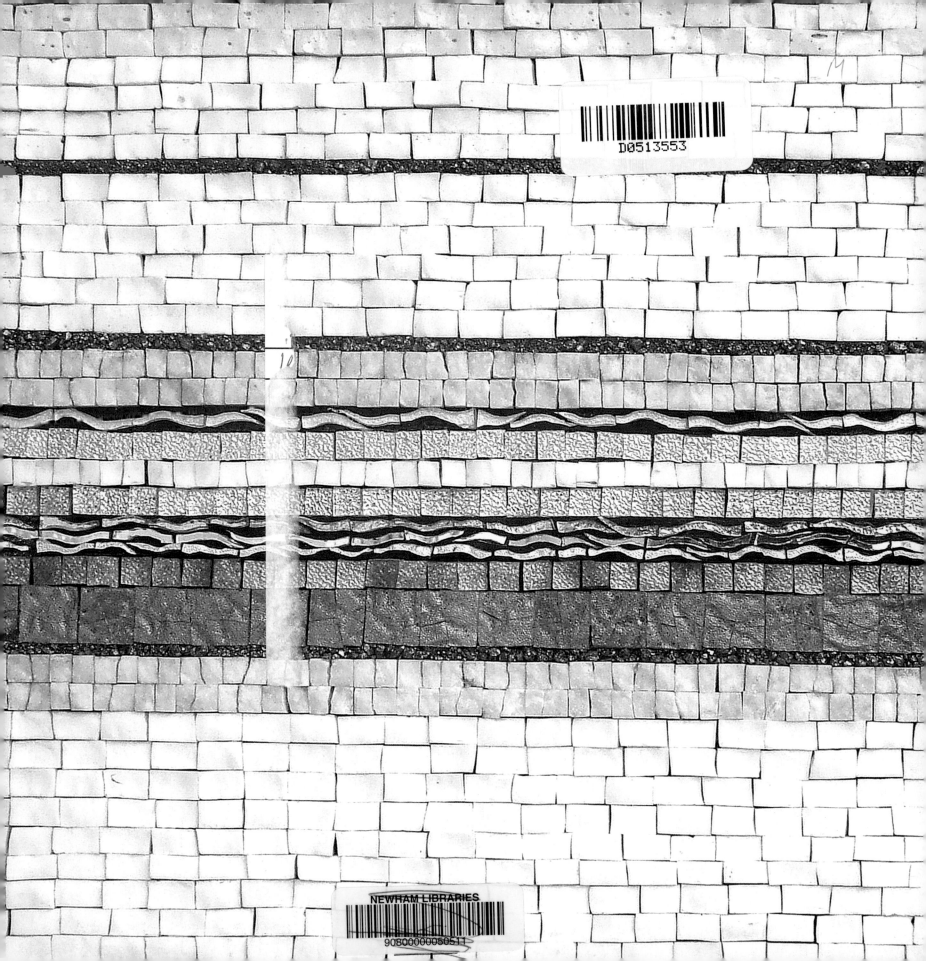

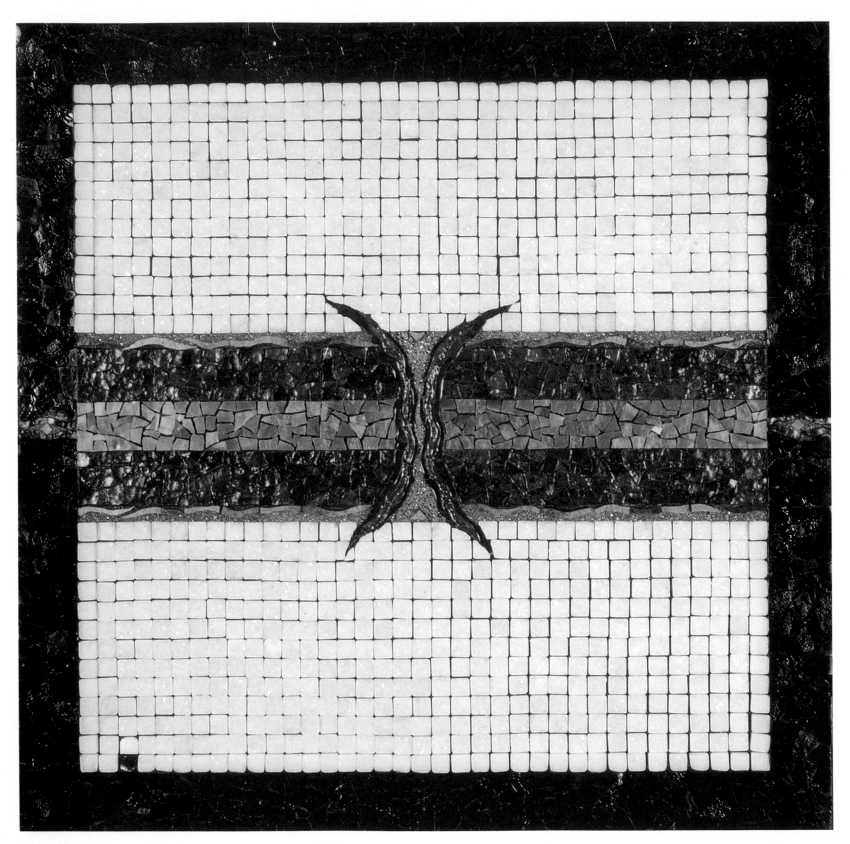

Hold Me Again (Fire), *2008, Elaine M. Goodwin, Carrara marble, Venetian gold, Ravenna mirror glass, smalti*

# Mosaic Today

Create contemporary projects using new and recycled material

## Elaine M Goodwin

**DAVID PORTEOUS**

CHUDLEIGH · DEVON

## Dedication

A celebration:
To the "Loves" in my life
EMG

## Mosaic

The derivation of the word is not historically secure, but it is inspiring to think that it comes directly, or even indirectly, from the Muses.

## Mosaic: the Definition

An art work: composed of individual loosely-defined three dimensional elements – called tesserae – which have most often been cut, chosen and positioned on a surface in a specific way to create a coherent design or image, where the gaps also play a role. When secure and completed it can be permanently sited or moved at will.

"The only way to create a mosaic… is to think mosaic when you are producing it"

Lucio Orsoni, 2000

## Acknowledgements

I thank warmly all the many museum curators and directors who graciously permitted pictures of their valued treasures for this publication. Also, I gratefully acknowledge all the photography used in this publication, including where permissions were exhaustively searched for to no avail. I thank also those collectors who allowed inclusion of their work

I am indebted to Lindy Ayubi for her painstaking patience in transcribing and in some cases translating my copiously scribbled notes, jottings and diagrams into the pristine elegance of a legible script – my heartfelt thanks. To Jules, my Puck of a photographer, dexterously photographing each work in a variety of light settings and sequences, as well as accompanying me to record images in a number of countries. Her good humor is as unwavering as her camera is forever moving – thank you. For proofreading and adding an index I extend to Jane Clark my warmest thanks. And to my publisher, David Porteous, for his accommodating suggestions and support, and who has on occasion been known to wield a drill in the fixing of a mosaic design or two! Many thanks.

In addition, Bardo Museum, Tunisia; Birmingham Museum and Art Gallery, England; British Museum, London, England; Carthage Museum, Tunisia; Hatay Museum, Antakya, Turkey; El Jem Museum, Tunisia; Louvre Museum, Paris, France; Naples Archaeological Museum, Italy; Pergamon Museum Berlin, Germany; Österreichische Museum für Angewandte Kunst, Vienna, Austria; Dr Mehmet Önal and Gaziantep Museum, Turkey; Sanliurfa Museum, S. E. Anatolia, Turkey; Sousse Museum, Tunisia; Amanath; Glencairn Balfour-Paul; Richard Bent; Bob Buntin; Paolo di Buono, and the Studio of Mosaic, Vatican City; Samir Chebki; Les Clifton; Nicole Depeu; Robert Field; Rama Goodwin; the late Arthur Goodwin; Filiz Hosukoglu; John Melville; Aylin Tan; Henri Wies; Thomas Landscapes, Exeter.

Finally I extend an enormous thank you to all my artist friends world-wide who contributed in so many ways to this publication. We know mosaic is a vibrant and vital part of our cultural experience today, and hope through our work this will extend to many others...

### Photo Credits

All the photographs for this book are taken by "Jules" (Karen Taylor) unless otherwise stated (www.karentaylorphotographer.co.uk).

### Contributing artists' websites

*Gazanfer Bayram* www.bayram.org.mk
*Gérard Brand* www.amagalerie.com/g.brand
*Elaine M. Goodwin* www.elainemgoodwin.co.uk
*Ilia Iliev* www.stamengrigorov.org email:ilievi_art@mail.bg
*Toyoharu Kii* www1.ttv.ne.jp/~sosos/index.html
*Sonia King* www.mosaicworks.com email:sonia@mosaicowrks.com
*Edda Mally* www.edda-mally.at email:eddamally@hotmail.com
*Catherine Mandron* www.cathymandron.com
*Josie Martin* www.linton.co.nz email:josiemartin@paradise.net.nz
*Anna Minardo* www.annaminardo.com
*Jan O'highway* www.janohighway.com email:info@janohighway.com
*Ilana Shafir* www.shafirart.com email:artilana@012.net.il
*George Trak* www.trakart.org email:artcentre@abv.bg
*Isaiah Zagar* www.isaiahzagar.org email:info@isaiahzagar.com

A CiP catalogue record for this book is available from the British Library.

ISBN 978-1-870586-55-9

Published by David Porteous Editions,
PO Box 5, Chudleigh, Newton Abbot,
Devon, TQ13 0YZ

www.davidporteous.com

Printed in Singapore by Star Standard.

### Safety Notice

Mosaic making can be dangerous, and readers should follow safety procedures and wear protective clothing and goggles at all times during the preparation of tesserae and the making and fitting of mosaics. The author, copyright holders and publishers of this book cannot accept legal liability for any damage or injury sustained as a result of making mosaics.

*Endpapers:* Lagoon Lights, *2004, detail, by Elaine M Goodwin*

# Contents

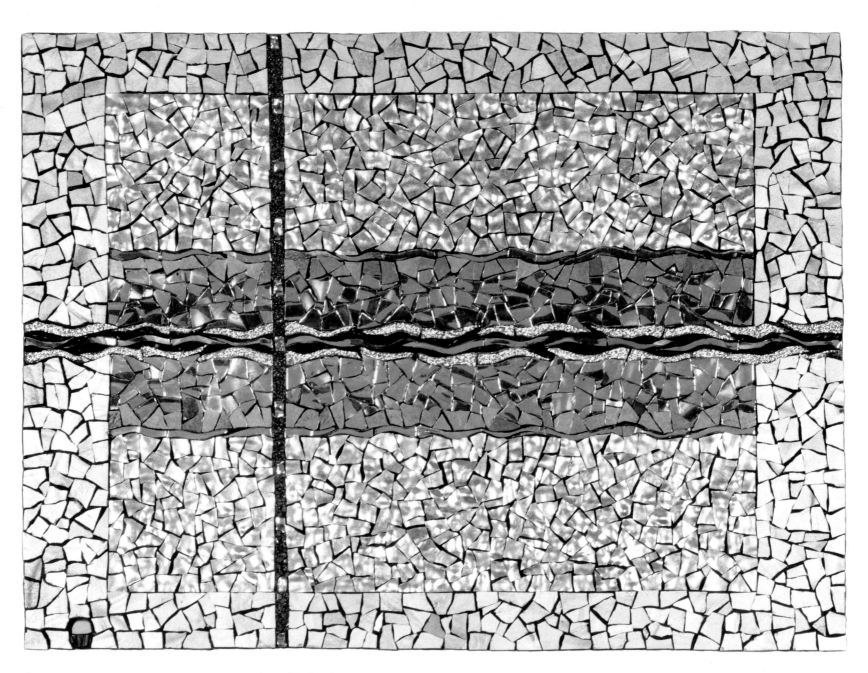

Come Lie with Me and be my Love I, *2007, Elaine M. Goodwin*

# Introduction

This book aims to illustrate a sense of the immediate in the creative world of mosaic today. Mosaic, like its characteristic surface, is a multifaceted art form. Its many areas of expression together form a very strong, very beautiful, and very leading position in the visual arts. Yet each individual facet which makes up the medium has its own unique identity.

For this publication, therefore, I have chosen to explain four naturally-occurring facets of mosaic – the decorative and ornamental; the exterior and garden; the experimental and enquiring; and the personal and self-expressive.

Mosaic as a decorative art form is the most known and has by far the most practicing adherents today – from the mosaic initiate to the acknowledged professional – and it also has the longest history. The other three facets I have chosen to illustrate have a number of devotees who are developing the mosaic medium into one of extraordinary richness, diversity and profundity.

To further illustrate the four facets I have asked twenty highly-esteemed artists from around the world, who are passionate professionals in one area or another, to create wherever possible a new work specially for this book and to share something of their present philosophy or technique. This, I hope, will give greater insight into the versatility and vitality of this wonderful medium of mosaic.

It may be that the artists straddle more than one aspect of mosaic – the facets of mosaic work frequently intermingle and reflect off one another for added coherence and illumination.

The sixteen designs created for teaching reference and inspiration reveal to the reader/maker some of the intricacies, techniques and secrets of mosaic making in progressive steps. With knowledge of the inspiration behind each design, it is hoped a greater understanding into the medium can be gained – an art form which has through six millennia developed and is continuing to develop unique, beautiful and enduring expressions to enhance our lives today.

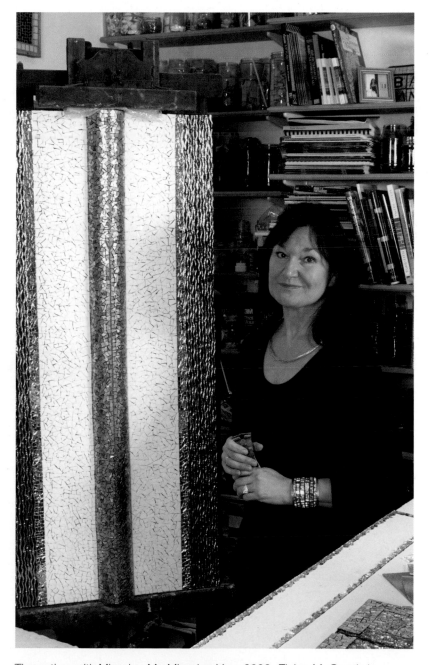

*The author with* Mirroring Me Mirroring You, *2006, Elaine M. Goodwin*

# In the Studio/Workspace

## The Workspace

The medium of mosaic is an obsessive medium; one which makes demands on time, skill and an enquiring mind. It can challenge in so many ways – the most basic of which is where to work. Ideally the workspace should be as permanent as you can make it – a spare room, a garage, a garden shed or outhouse, or a studio – you will want to spend more and more time in it. Once claimed, essentials include:

1. good lighting – from a natural or adequate artificial source (daylight bulbs are preferred by many artists);
2. good storage – for displaying and storing tools and materials;
3. good workbench – the chair or stool should be of a complementary height to the desk as a posture may be held for a long time;
4. good ventilation, access to water, and a space, preferably an exterior one, for the grouting and washing of mosaics.

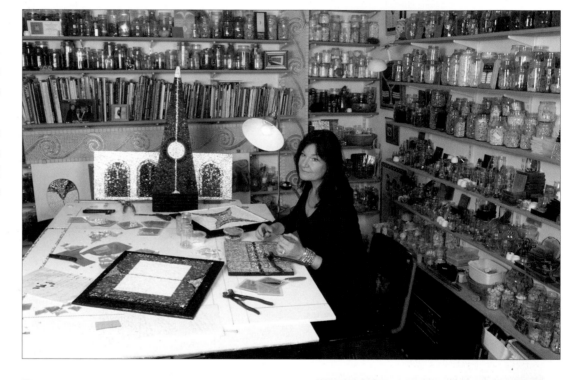

*The studio workspace should be personalized to your way of working, and have, if possible, flexibility to accommodate various techniques of mosaic making, at an easel (below left) or at a workbench.*

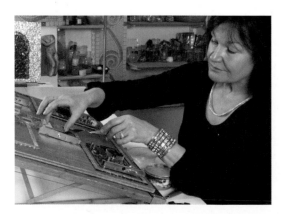

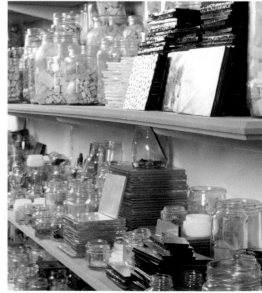

*Right: Strong shelving is essential for holding the materials to be used in mosaic.*

# Materials

*The materials as they appear in sequence within a frame of single uncut and unglazed black mosaic tiles:*

unglazed ceramic mosaic tiles – blue, green mottled;
unglazed ceramic floor mosaic tiles – green;
glazed and metallic-glazed mosaic tiles – reds;
vitreous glass mosaic tiles – orange, yellow, green, blue;
*smalti*; handmade Venetian mosaic glass – pale yellow;
vitreous glass mosaic tiles with added copper dust – violet, green;
vitreous glass mosaic tiles – indigo;
*smalti / smalti antico*; handmade Venetian mosaic glass – indigo, violet;
*smalti trasparenti* hand-made Venetian mosaic glass – which have been placed on a silver-painted backing board to accent the color;
Ravenna mirror glass – deep gold, pale gold, orange, pale green, silver, pale blue; plain Venetian gold-leaf – red, green, violet;
Venetian gold-leaf used in reverse – metallic turquoise blue;
granulated Venetian gold-leaf;
Venetian gold-leaf floor glass;
stained glass – metallic purple;
*millefiori* – blue / yellow;
shells – natural white cockle shells;
opalized glass – green / blue;
abalone – cut from the interior of a shell;
china – blue and white willow pattern;
agate – striated blues;

The central panel is defined with cubes of Carrara white marble. It contains samples of:
mother of pearl;
granite;
plain silver-backed mirror glass
cut-glass jewel;
Venetian white gold-leaf glass;
Biancone marble;
gray slate;
sea-washed green and white bottle glass;
small white pebbles.

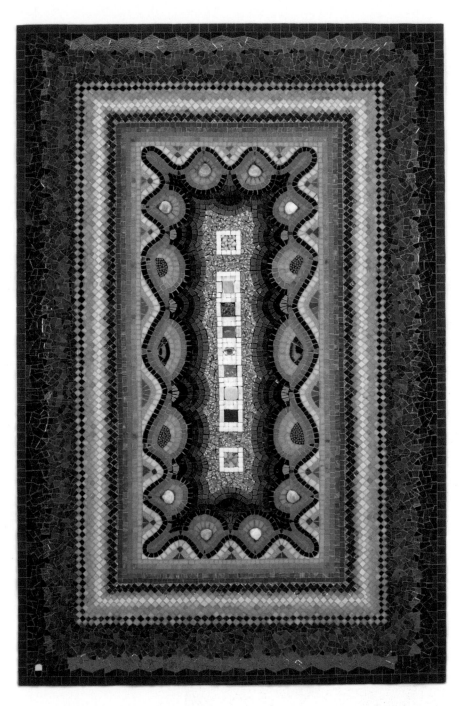

*Materials Panel*: A panel of the most commonly used mosaic materials, laid in a rainbow of color from red to violet. The work also incorporates examples of the laying methods used in mosaic making – the *opera*.

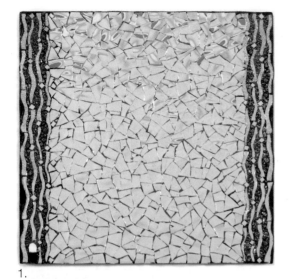

1.

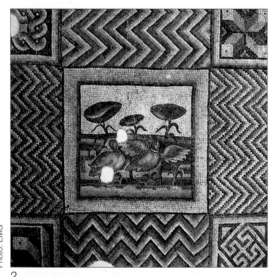

Photo: EMG

2.

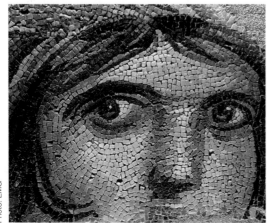

Photo: EMG

3.

# Opera

The word most commonly used for the mosaic making unit is *tessera* (pl. *tesserae*); occasionally you will see the words *tessellae* or *tesserulae*. The tesserae may be laid in various ways called *opera*.

**1.** Mists III, *2007, Elaine M Goodwin*
**opus palladianum**: the tesserae are cut into random shapes and articulated to form a crazy paving effect.

**2.** *Geometric border; rainbow cable with Fish, Ducks, Lotuses, 5th century, Daphne. Hatay Archaeological Museum, Antioch / Antakya, Turkey*
**opus reticulatum**: the tesserae are cut into squares and are laid on their points. This forms a textural effect, sometimes termed a 'rainbow cable', as the colors are optically mixed from a distance.

**3.** *Maened/female face, 2nd century AD, Gaziantep Museum, Turkey*
**opus vermiculatum**: the tesserae are laid in successive lines to outline a particular form or image. By contouring in this way, a sense of articulation or movement is created.

**4.** *Little Bird, before 79 AD, Pompeii, Italy*
**opus tessellatum**: the tesserae are cut in fairly regular square or cube shapes and laid in either horizontal or vertical lines, forming a strong ground.

**5.** Black and White, *by Victor Vasarely, 1960. Musée de la Mosaïque, Briare, France*
**opus regulatum**: the tesserae are laid in uniform lines of square-shaped tesserae, forming a strong formalized pattern.

**6.** *Geometric mosaic, detail, 5th century, Hatay Museum Antioch / Antakya, Turkey*
**Shell / scallop opus**: the tesserae are laid in a pattern to form a scallop shape and then filled.

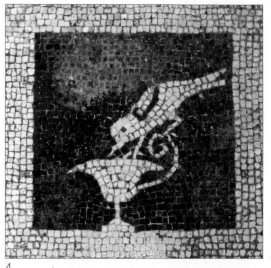

Photo: EMG

4.

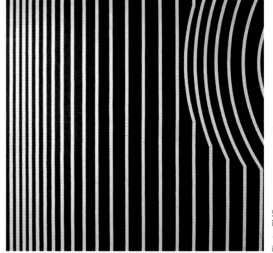

Photo: EMG

5.

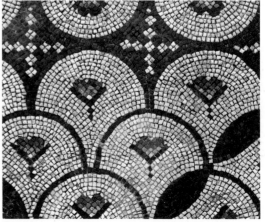

Photo: EMG

6.

# Tools: Hand-held Mosaic Nippers

Illustrations of the most frequently used tools for cutting mosaic. Each image shows how to hold both the mosaic cutting tool and the material.

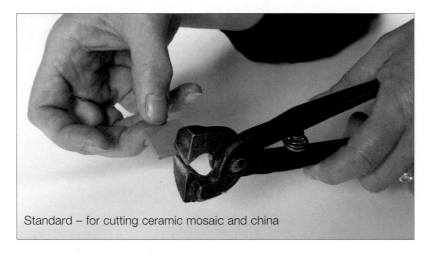

Standard – for cutting ceramic mosaic and china

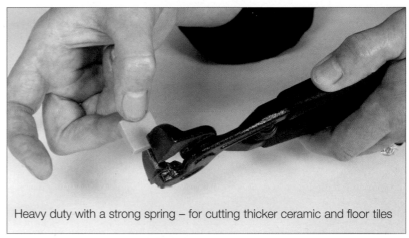

Heavy duty with a strong spring – for cutting thicker ceramic and floor tiles

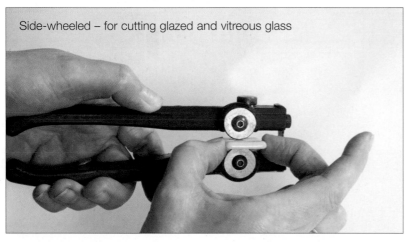

Side-wheeled – for cutting glazed and vitreous glass

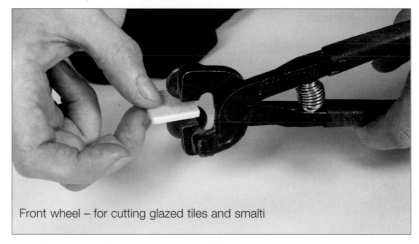

Front wheel – for cutting glazed tiles and smalti

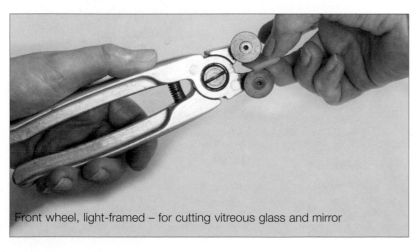

Front wheel, light-framed – for cutting vitreous glass and mirror

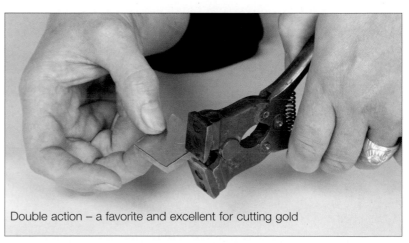

Double action – a favorite and excellent for cutting gold

## Hammer and Hardie

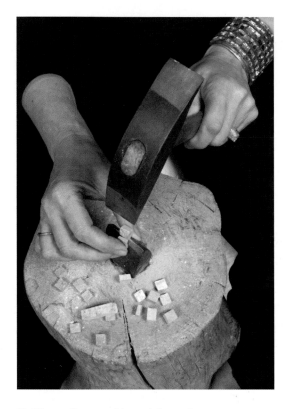

*Cutting yellow marble* – giallo reale

## Glass Cutter and Glass Pliers

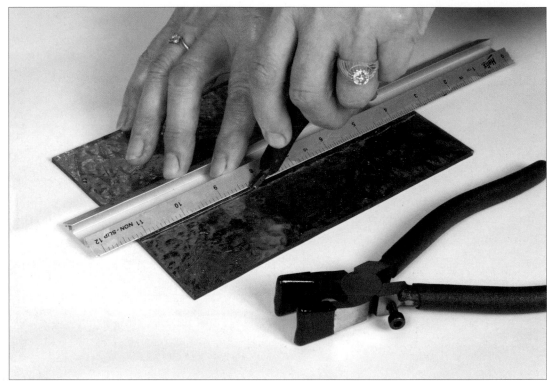

*Scoring golden yellow mirror glass which will then be pressed along the scored line, using the glass pliers to form a clean break. Tile cutters, saws, pliers and other cutting tools can also be utilized to create the tesserae for application in mosaic.*

# Adhesives

The most common adhesives are water-based *polyvinyl acetates (PVA)* or their equivalents, commonly called *white glues*; cements of various kinds; and *epoxy resins*. All have excellent adhesive properties and are used according to the porosity of the materials and the situations.

- PVA or white glues bond tesserae to all forms of timber, i.e., where at least one surface is porous.
- Cements are excellent for external situations and direct applications of tesserae at site.
- Epoxy resins are used in situations of high humidity, in watery conditions, or when the tesserae
  are to be bonded to plastic or metal surfaces or to other non-porous materials.

A variety of other adhesives may be used from time to time, for example, *gum arabic* or *paper glue*.

# Grouts

As well as the traditional grouts of sand and cement – in their various colors and proprietary and personal combinations – other materials will find themselves employed in a 'grouting' capacity, e.g., fool's gold (iron pyrites), glass frit, coarse and fine sands and gravels, and even decorative substances used in the garden and design industry. Many permanent crushable materials with enduring characteristics can be employed for mosaic use.

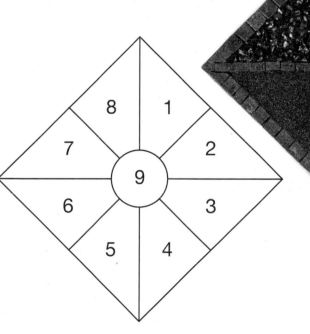

1. fine-grained white frit or glass granules
2. very fine dark red sand (collected from Egypt)
3. ochre-colored gravels
4. medium-grained black frit or glass granules
5. decorative gray granules
6. *pozzolana* – volcanic ash (collected from Southern Italy)
7. coarse metallic-red granules
8. alabaster fragments (collected from Egypt)
9  clear ground glass

## Other Equipment

Other equipment used in a mosaic workspace can include backing timber, brushes, desk easels, fiber netting, drawing paper, brown paper, palette knives, ruler and measures, pencils, crayons, markers and other drawing implements, compasses, protractor, and many, many containers, with or without lids, for holding both materials and adhesives, and all the hundred and one other objects which are sure to be accumulated as work in mosaic progresses.

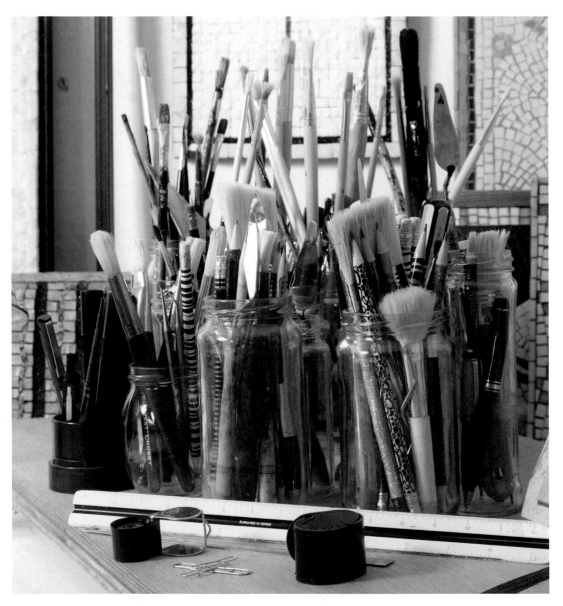

*Jars containing pencils and palette knives, brushes, prodders and other useful objects for mosaic making.*

## Safety

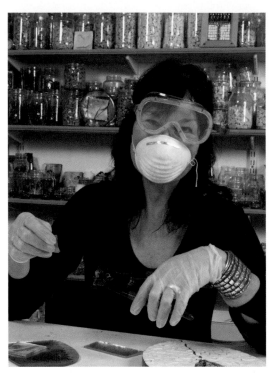

*Protect yourself well, when making mosaics!*

Being aware of all possible safety precautions is a very crucial part of all mosaic making.

When cutting it is important at all times to wear protective glasses or goggles. Latex or rubber gloves must be worn whenever acids, cements or epoxy glues are used, and whenever it is felt that the hands need protection from any potentially harmful substances or cutting procedures. Dust masks and nose and mouth filters are necessary to help eliminate the dust which is an inevitable side effect of many of the mosaic processes, e.g., cutting, mixing cement, etc. It is therefore advisable that at all times and throughout all procedures, thorough attention is given to the highest safety and security measures – when in doubt, self-protect.

# Decorative and Ornamental

## Historical Viewpoints

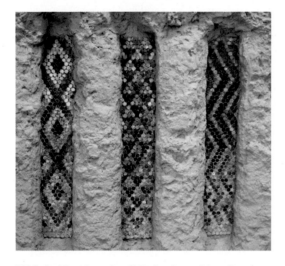

*Wall designs, temple of Warka, Iraq, 4th millennium BCE. Pergamon Museum, Berlin, Germany*

It is generally accepted that the decorative walls of a temple, whose fragmented remains can be seen in the Pergamon Museum of Berlin, Germany, form what is thought to be the earliest acknowledged example of what can be called mosaic.

Cone-shaped units of around 2-4in / 5-10cm have been pressed tightly together into a simple mortar of fired clay or gypsum. Their exposed, flat heads, approximately ½in/1.5cm in diameter, are painted in colors of black, white and terracotta to form striking geometric patterns of simple, strong design. The patterns consist of zig-zags, lozenges, triangles and other basic geometrical shapes, in imitation of textiles or matting. It is indeed aesthetically pleasing.

Units cut into shapes then become part

of a long history of design and appear under a wide variety of headings:

*Opus sectile*

This is a form of mosaic where marble, colored stones and other materials are cut to predetermined shapes as part of a geometric, figurative or patterned design, forming an inlay. This type of work is most commonly found in geometric or ornamental pavement designs, frequently made of bright, polychrome materials.

A more refined form is used for figure-work on walls or on small objects.

*Intarsia / Tarsia*:  This form of mosaic may use a wide variety of materials, including marble, ivory, mother of pearl, or metal. The design is engraved onto a surface and the material laid into it, the supporting wood or backing material often becoming part of the design. It results in a patterned flat surface, often of great complexity.

But true mosaic, as we acknowledge it

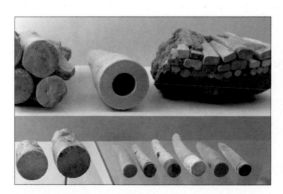

*Examples of the cone shapes used for wall mosaic. Warka, (Ancient Erech), Iraq, Pergamon Museum, Berlin, Germany*

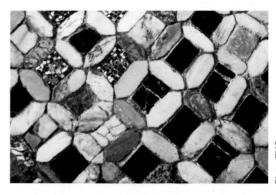

Opus Sectile;  *floor detail, S. Maria Assunta, Torcello, Venice, Italy, early 11th-13th century*

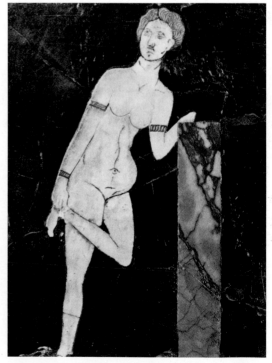

Opus sectile; *colored marbles, Aphrodite putting on her sandal, 12½in x 9½i / 33cm x 24cm, Pompeii, Archaeological Museum, Naples, Italy*

Photo: EMG

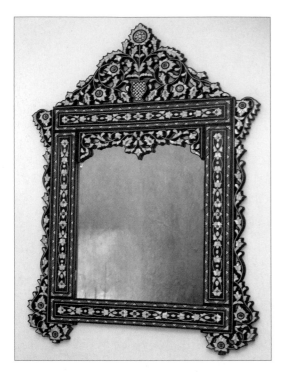

Intarsia: *A contemporary ornamental mirror, Morocco, mother-of-pearl and abalone*

today, has its roots in the pebble mosaics of the Mediterranean. Very early examples of pebbles used for decorative flooring and paving have been found in Turkey, and in south-western Sicily, Italy. However, it is at Pella in Greece that a wondrous flowering of decorative -borders can best be seen.

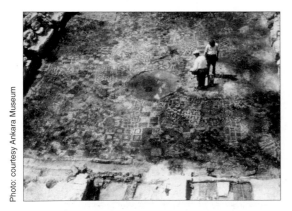

*Pebble mosaic 8th century, BCE, Gordium, Phrygia, Central Asia Minor, Turkey*

Pella is noted particularly for its figurative designs – but these are all framed with borders of great beauty and intricacy. They are complex and suggest a three-dimensional aspect and they are glorious. Drawn with white pebbles on a black ground, they twist and turn with floral abandon.

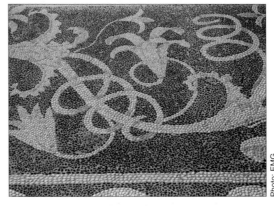

*Decorative floral scroll pattern, 4th century BCE, Pella, Macedonia, Greece*

This Hellenistic device of drawing an image in white or pale colors on a dark or black ground, evolved into a highly sophisticated mosaic technique where cubes of marble and stone were used to form decorative floor designs.

The Greek mosaicists developed mosaic as skillful and polychromatic 'paintings', manipulating the tiny units of mosaic in order to

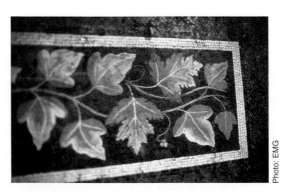

*Detail, Hellenistic mosaic, 1st century BCE, Archaeological Museum, Aquiliea, northern Italy*

deceive the eye – they were not paintings.

An artist made famous for his highly complex and painterly mosaic technique was Sosos, from Pergamon in Turkey, who worked in the 2nd century BCE. His work was extremely fine and realistic, and was greatly admired. It is copied, even to the present day, particularly versions of his unswept floors.

The spread of the succeeding Roman Empire gave rise to an increasing number of villas and baths (*domus* and *thermae*) which needed flooring, resulting in mosaics of both monochromatic and polychromatic beauty. A huge repertoire of designs emerged. The Romans turned the Hellenistic painterly fascination with ornamental intricacy into one of simpler figurative and geometric intrigue or formalized patterning. Often the designs were visually textural, like carpets.

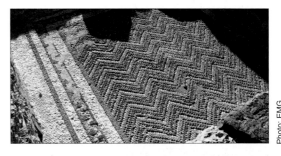

*Geometric flooring, House of Neptune, 3rd century AD, Thuburbo Majus, Tunisia*

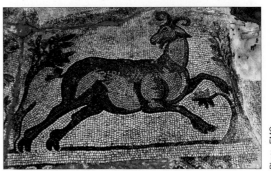

*Animal Mosaic, 2nd century AD, detail, Sanliurfa Museum, Turkey*

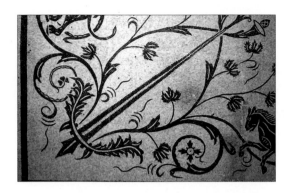

*Black and white pavement, detail, Ostia, Italy, 1st-2nd century AD, Pergamon Museum, Berlin, Germany*

Alongside these more abstract rug-like designs, motifs of vines, flowers, garlands, animals, fish and trees appeared, all delighting in their decorative aspects, so appropriate for mosaic.

The symbolism of the images depicted in these Roman mosaics is eternal, repeated throughout centuries and cultures, and adapted continuously for best contemporary understanding.

Thus, from the simplest black and white floors popular in the 1st/2nd century of late Republican Rome, as seen in the maritime port of

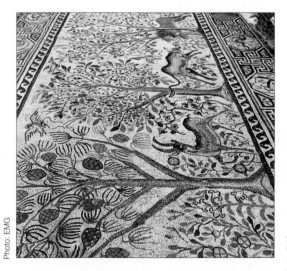

*Mosaic floor, detail, Heraklea, 3rd-4th century AD, near Bitola, Macedonia.*

Ostia Antica, to the all-over carpet floors of the Roman Empire, mosaic was widely acknowledged not only as a medium providing a practical floor covering but intrinsically as one of great beauty and decorative innovation.

The new religions of Christianity and Islam were to add significantly to this decorative pantheon. The mosaics of the 7-8th century mosque at Jerusalem, Israel, and the 8th century Great Ummayad mosque in Damascus, Syria, are richly decorated in smalti and gold with imagery of trees and leaves and fruit.

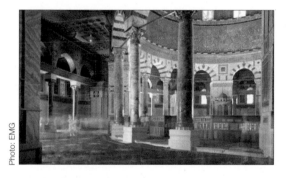

*Dome of the Rock, interior detail, 7-8th century, Jerusalem, Israel*

The mosaics in the *mihrab* of Cordoba continued this tradition into the 10th century.

In Christian buildings, the internal architectural features of window and arch soffits were

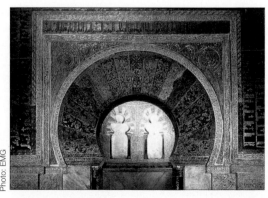

*Mihrab, mosque, 10th century, Cordoba, Spain*

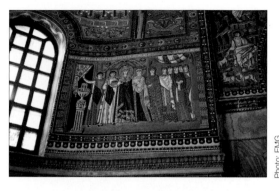

*Empress Theodora and her entourage, 6th century, San Vitale, Ravenna, Italy*

encrusted with mosaic patterning. From the 5th century onward, the walls of Byzantine-influenced churches, the domes and apses, exhibited superb examples of decorative mosaic work. Acknowledged centers including Ravenna, Venice, and Sicily, established mosaic as an ornamental and propagandizing art form *par excellence*.

## Other mosaic-related techniques
*Zellij – Moroccan tiles*
A facet of mosaic-making also emerging from around the 10-11th centuries was the tile mosaic – *zellij* – so prolific in Islamic Northern Africa, particularly Morocco. Here each tile takes a shape and a name, e.g. four clasped hands, spider's

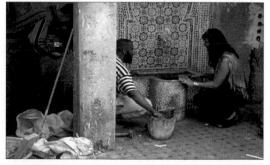

*The author and the zellij master (zlayji) regard a newly-finished wall fountain which used a simple 8-point star pattern as the inspirational design*

house, and are pieced together in an infinity of variations to form stunningly beautiful designs of great meditative strength.

### Cosmati

There can be no denying that pattern and decoration play a seminal and satisfying role in visual artistic development under the title of mosaic making.

The style known as Cosmati or Cosmatesque, originated in Rome in the early 12th century and spread out to encompass much of Europe. It is a smooth-surfaced multi-colored mosaic form of decoration, underpinned with geometric rules.

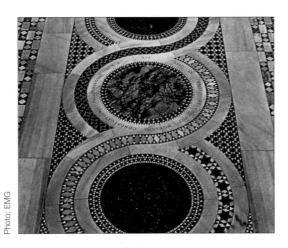

*Cosmati pavement, S. Prassede, Rome, italy, as made in 1927 after the original*

### Nineteenth and Twentieth Centuries

In Europe, the interest in decorating churches with large amounts of decorative mosaic work continued well into the late 15th century, but there followed a period of indifference and malaise which relegated mosaic to picture copying. This continued up to a time of reinvigorated attention in the mid-19th century in Europe and England. This renewed awareness was encouraged by the

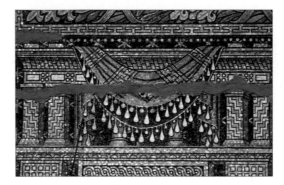

*Kaiser Wilhelm Memorial Church, detail, ornamental ceilng coving, 1895, Berlin, Germany*

newly-created factory-made vitreous glass and ceramic tiles.

In Germany the neo-Byzantine mosaics in the hall of the Kaiser Wilhelm memorial church are richly decorative and luminous. They were designed by Hermann Schaper (1853-1911) as watercolors and carried out by the esteemed mosaic firm of Puhl and Wagner in Berlin, which operated from 1889 to 1969.

The Cathedral of Aachen possesses c. 2989 square yards / 2,500 square meters of mosaic work, carried out from 1880 to 1913. Although restored, the mosaics are able to emit something of the decorative splendor of the original.

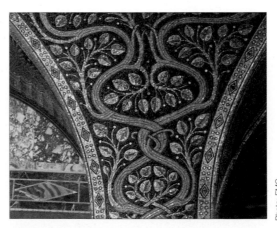

*Spandrel decoration, 19th century, Aachen Cathedral, Germany*

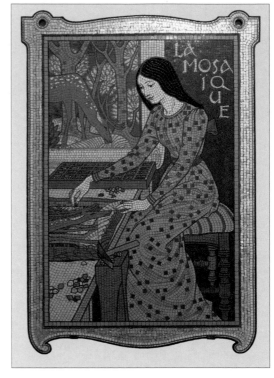

La Mosaïque, *1895, Eugène Grasset, Musée de la Mosaïque et des Emaux de Briare, France*

In France, at Briare, the mosaic work of the Swiss artist Eugène Grasset (1845-1917) can be seen throughout the town, in the church, the hospital, and in the Museum of *Mosaïque et des Emaux.*

Also in France, in Paris, is the Pasteur Institute, which holds the tomb of the great scientist Louis Pasteur (d. 1895). The tomb is located in the crypt of the building – a space decorated extensively with mosaic in a neo-Byzantine / Art Nouveau style by Auguste Guilbert-Martin (1825-1900).

In England and also in Ireland, the artist Eric Newton (1893-1965) designed a great number of mosaics for his grandfather's established mosaic firm of Ludwig Oppenheimer (1865-1965). The workshop was heavily influenced by the Italian mosaics of Ravenna and Venice, and those in

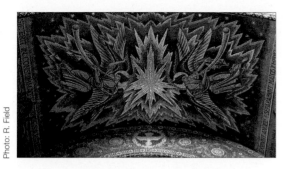

*Two Angels, detail, Church of St John the Baptist, Rochdale, England, 1930-33*

Istanbul, Turkey, particularly Hagia Sophia. Most notable from their prolific output is the mosaic scheme for the Church of St John the Baptist in Rochdale, England.

The Russian artist Boris Anrep (1855-1969) moved to London, England in 1911. He worked on many mosaics in the city, for public buildings including Westminster Cathedral (1956-1962), the National Gallery, the Tate Gallery, and for private commissions.

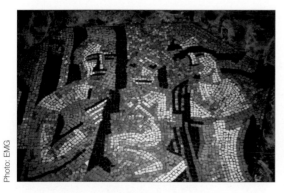

*Detail, from* Various Moments in the Day of a Lady of Fashion, *1922, Boris Anrep; Birmingham Museum and Art Gallery, England*

### The 1950s
In the late 1950s and 1960s, with the onset of Op-Art and the computer age, mosaics appeared with a strictly geometrical optical effect. Most memo-

rable is the work of Victor Vasarely (1908-1997). Vasarely was born in Pecs, Hungary, and trained at the Bauhaus-influenced Mohély Academy, Budapest. From 1931 he made his home in Paris where he worked using a system of grids in contrasting colors, creating optical illusions. He was naturally drawn to manufactured mosaic, where the elemental shape of the square with its scaled color spectrum allowed an infinite number of optical color combinations.

The decorative approach to mosaic remains at the forefront. Mosaicists worldwide are drawn to the medium for its decorative potential and lasting universal beauty and practicality.

# Inspirations from Contemporary Artists

The following renowned mosaicists create distinctly textural mosaics of rich color and form, or pronounced movement (*andamento*) – all of which are highly refined features of their contemporary decorative works. Each artist's work is a personal interpretation, adding new vigor to the long history of applied and decorative mosaic work.

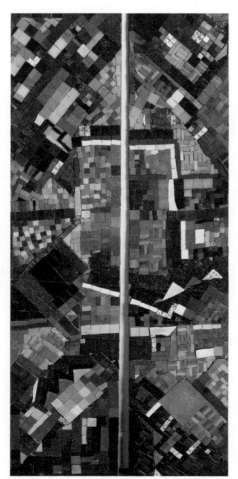

### Ketty Abdel-Malek
Born in Alexandria, Egypt, 1930s. Lives and works in Cairo, Egypt.

*Artist's Statement, Cairo, Egypt, 2007*
Mosaic – what a wonderful word. Mosaics of thoughts, of colors, of philosophy; the word implies such a mixture of art and yet is so particular.

Mosaic is first of all self expression. Every artist has a style, their own way of dealing with the stone. For me the stone is alive – it obeys if you gently manipulate it, yet it has a mind of its own.

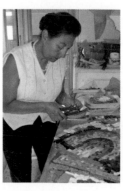

***Africa***, 2007, 39½in x 24in / 100cm x 62cm, vitreous glass, Venetian plain and rippled gold leaf glass, smalti

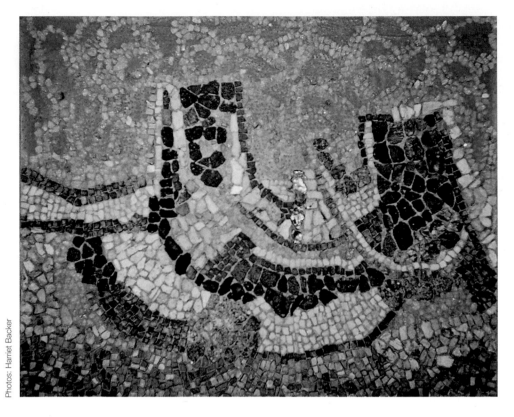

Photos: Harriet Backer

**Harriet Backer**
Born Oslo, Norway, 1934.  Lives and works in Oslo, Norway, and Malaga, Spain.

*Artist's Statement, Oslo. Norway,, 2007*
All my life I have made mosaics and I hope to continue to do so for the rest of my life.  I always return to Nature. I work with natural stones – like the world's first mosaics.  I think I am the first to make a mosaic with stones from the South Pole.  Each stone is inspiring in itself.

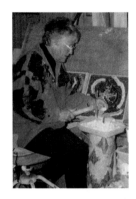

***Stones from the South Pole***, 2007, 47in x 32in / 120cm x 80 cm, natural  stones, blue grout

**Manfred Hoehn**
Born Wuerzburg, Germany, 1935. Lives and works in Oberhaching, Germany

*Artist's Statement, Oberhaching, Germany, 2007*
When I first joined the well-known Franz Mayer mosaic studios I was stunned by their completely new way of making mosaic.  Conceived by Professor Paul Knappe, it seemed a revolutionary understanding of applying all kinds of mosaic materials.  This system completely forms my own way of making contemporary mosaic, i.e., the initial selection and application of the materials – a highly intellectual act in itself – must be made *before* executing a mosaic.

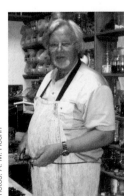

Photos: A. M. Hoehn

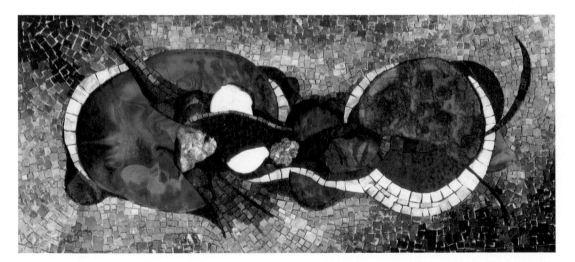

***Interpretation***, 2007, 43in x 20in / 50cm x 10cm, smalti, marble, smalti piastrina

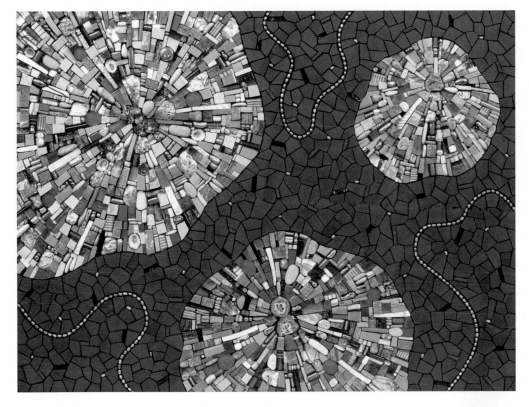

## Sonia King

Born in Texas, United States of America, in 1953. Lives and works in Dallas, Texas, United States of America.

*Artist's Statement, Texas, USA, 2007*
I create art to express the way I see the world; how it is and how it could be. I put together the tangible and intangible, bits of color and texture, fragments of meaning. My art is strongly related to a sense of place and a connection to the land, seeing the terrain in terms of its geology and topography. I want viewers to look at the world around them with different eyes after seeing my work.

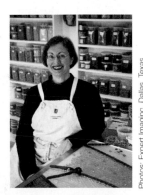

**Spin Off**, 2007,
18in x 24in / 51cm x70cm,
ceramic, glass, smalti, and
semi-precious stones

Photos: Expert Imaging, Dallas, Texas

## Alexander Vasiliev

Born South Kazakhstan region USSR, 1951. Lives and works in St Petersburg, Russia.

*Artist's Statement, St Petersburg, Russia, 2007*
I work in two different aspects of mosaic, one religious, the other secular. My religious work is inspired by early Byzantine mosaics: I work with fresco, mosaics and icons in Russian Orthodox churches in Russia and the United States of America. My other work is for living; for example sculptures for office interiors, and for exhibitions. For me, mosaic is light, colors and to express a personal philosophy.

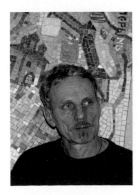

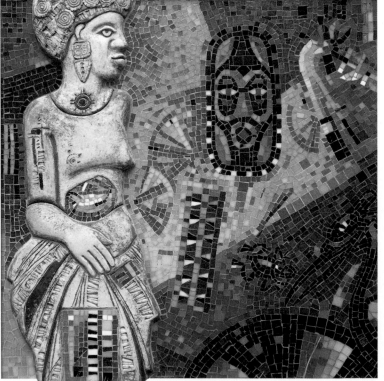

***Africa,*** 2005,
31½inx 31½in/ 80cm x 80cm,
ceramic relief, vitreous glass

Photos: Stas Vasiliev (the artist); the artist (Africa)

# Small Threshold Panel

## The Inspirational Mosaic

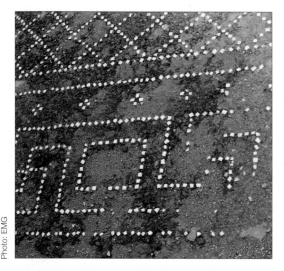

*Geometric flooring, detail, Ampurias, circa 1st century AD (Empúriesi, Emporion, founded circa 600 BC) north-east Spain*

## Background Revelations

There is something immensely satisfying about looking at patterns – repeated geometric motifs – as part of an overall design.

In Ampurias, where the floors are now roofless and left exposed to the light, the site can be enjoyed as a wonderful open air pattern book. There are many and varied designs to be seen with evolving pattern formations. It is pleasing to feel part of an early exploration of floor design development.

Very early on the itinerant Phoenicians and later the Greeks exploited geometric concepts to great and wondrous effect on the flooring of their residences in coastal areas of the Mediterranean.

With very minimalist reference to color and the merest of patterns, they created a weather proof flooring, skillfully balancing the functional with the aesthetic. They developed the simplest of mosaic ground covering, which is termed *opus signinum* (originating from the town of Segni in Italy, renowned for its rich red clay). This is a style of floor making which is called *cocciopesto* – literally one formed of baked clay. It is made up of a mortar of crushed terracotta tiles or burnt red-clay pottery, hydrated lime / lime water, and occasionally *pozzolana* – a volcanic lava added for its known damp and water resistance. This mix is laid and finished to a smooth surface.

Into it are pressed individual chippings, or tesserae, of white marble or occasionally alabaster. Sometimes tesserae of black or darker stone are added to form monochrome surface patternings. The designs can be seemingly unsophisticated, appearing as mere lines of simply-placed tesserae in running geometric patterns such as meanders or linked lozenges. Sometimes the tesserae are grouped into small decorative motifs, scattered at fairly regular intervals, over a larger area.

Yet so aesthetically pleasing and functionally sound is the result that this uncomplicated advancement of floor decoration lasted for some hundreds of years and is found in paving design from North Africa to Sicily and Southern Italy.

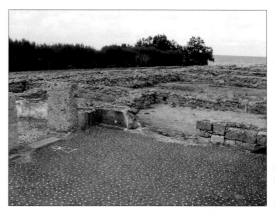

*Cocciopesto pavement, mid-3rd century BCE, Kerkouane, Tunisia (note the sign of Tanit, the Phoenician goddess, picked out in white marble)*

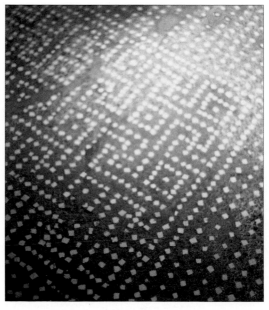

*Early morning light falling on a floor at Pompeii, 1st century AD*

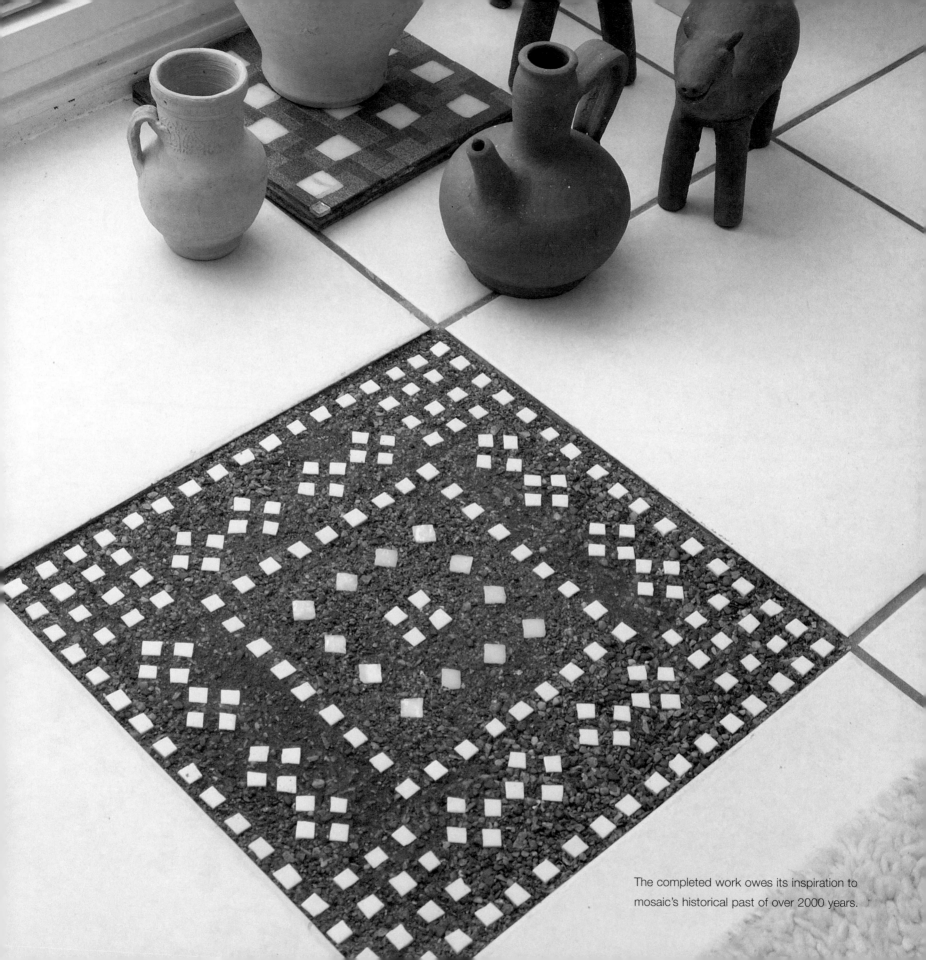

The completed work owes its inspiration to
mosaic's historical past of over 2000 years.

## Method

### The Drawing

Use a permanent red marker pen to strengthen the pencil-drawn tesserae which form the geometric pattern.

### Equipment

large sheet of drawing paper    eraser
red marker pen                  ruler
pencil

1 Measure the area to be worked in, and transfer these measurements to a large sheet of white paper. Use the pencil to devise a *simple* geometric pattern, made up of squares approximating to the size of individual tessera to be used. If it helps, construct a pencil grid of squares over the area, and work out a systematical design on this. When completed, firm up the drawn pattern of tesserae with a permanent marker pen.

### Preparing the site

### Equipment

ready-made cement mix    container
protective gloves        water
trowel

2 The site of the area to be worked on. The floor is composed of large white ceramic floor tiles set onto a concrete foundation. One tile has been left out and the foundation mortar smoothed to a fine finish. The very small size of the area to be filled, 13in x 13in / 33cm x 33cm in a

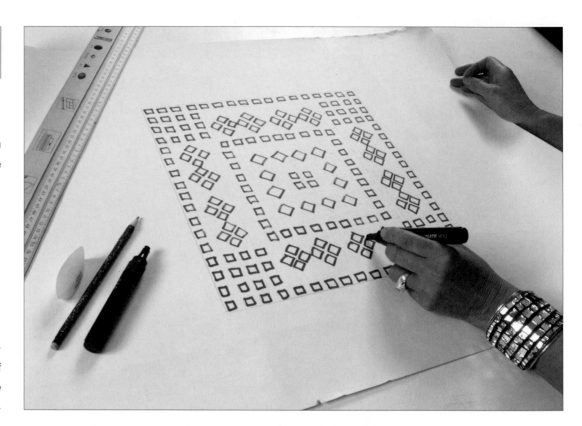

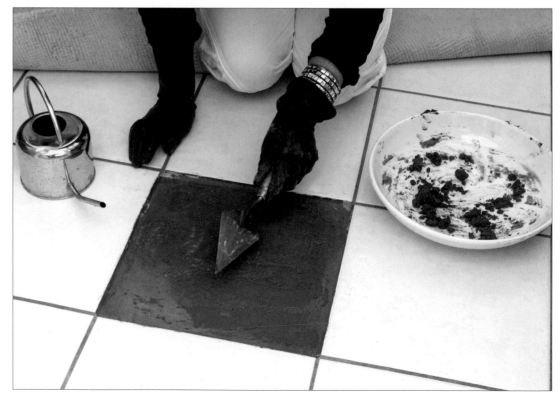

pre-determined site, calls for a variation of the normal *opus signinum* procedure. Here the tesserae will be laid first and the *cocciopesto* mortar added as a grout. If you are able to work in a larger area, invert the process – laying the textured mortar first in manageable sections, and 'pressing home' the tesserae in a chosen pattern.

The strength and appeal of *opus signinum* is its semi-spontaneous character. Do not be too exacting when cutting and placing the square-shaped tesserae. Any small irregularities will enliven the surface and avoid a deadening, mechanical quality.

## Materials

fiber netting

sheet of clear plastic

scissors

studio knife/Stanley knife

steel ruler

brushes

pva adhesive/white glue

palette knife

sticky tape /Scotch tape

glazed white ceramic tiles, ¾in x ¾in/20mm x 20mm

white luster glazed tiles, ¾in x ¾in/20mm x 20mm

drawing board (optional)

large tile (optional)

standard mosaic nippers

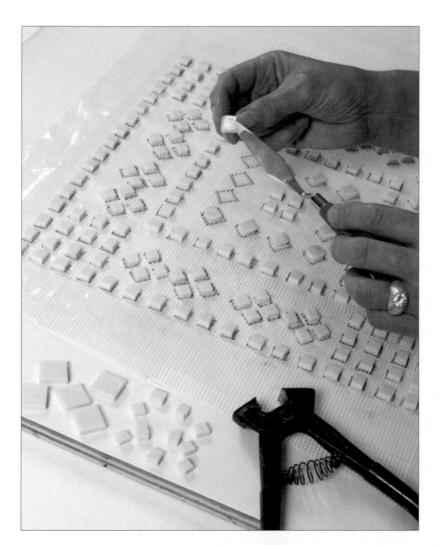

**3** Fixing a tessera onto the fiber netting to form a simple pattern. Cover the drawing with the sheet of clear plastic and fix it with the sticky tape at one end to a drawing board or work table. Cover this with a square of fiber netting and again fix it down at the same point. Having one fixed point only will allow the netting to be occasionally smoothed during the making process – as sometimes stretching or bunching can occur.

Cut the tiles into four and begin to adhere the tesserae to the fiber netting by putting a little of the adhesive on the back of each tessera, using the palette knife, and then placing it on the netting following the clearly seen drawn design.

The tesserae are not placed close to each other but some distance apart, with their smooth face uppermost. At some point in the design, fix a variant white tile – I have chosen a luster finish for an inner area which will add interest and bring to mind the use of other materials such as alabaster, occasionally seen in ancient *cocciopesto* floors.

When the design is completed, it is advisable to cover it with a heavy tile, to avoid displacement and ensure an even surface while it is drying. It is usually recommended to leave it for 24 hours to ensure the bonding.

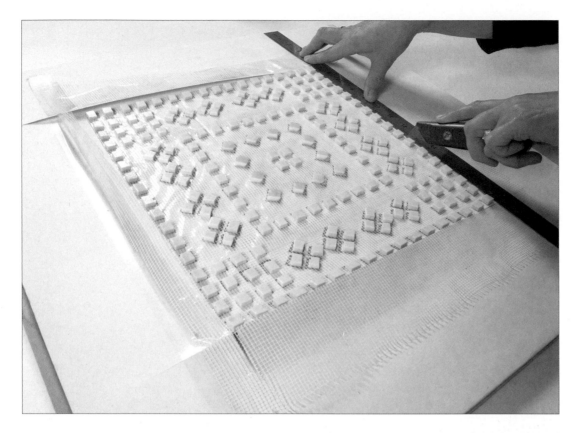

4 Using the studio knife to cut away the surplus fiber netting. When the tesserae are secure, gently release the netting from the plastic backing and lift the whole design and turn it over. Again, allow this to dry completely before cutting away the surplus netting to leave just the exact size to accommodate to the site.

5 Carry the design to the site. The site should be primed beforehand with neat pva or white glue, using a brush, before the mosaic on the net is gently laid in position. Leave to dry thoroughly.

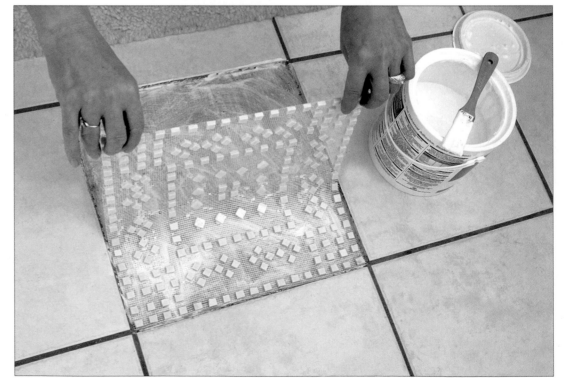

# Grouting: *cocciopesto* infill

## Materials

Proprietary gray grouting powder

white glue/pva adhesive

water

bowls or containers

coarse red gravel

deep red sand (I have used some collected In
   Mediterranean Tunisia)

small trowel

palette knife

plastic sheeting

large tile

cloths

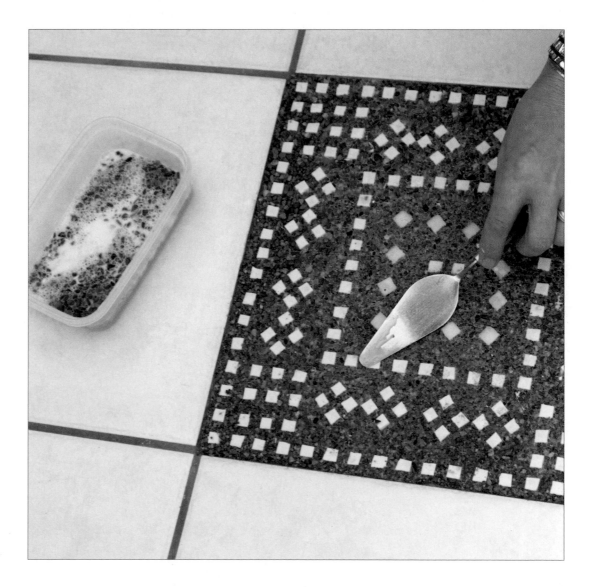

6 In a container thoroughly mix a quantity of gravel and sand with the proprietary cement grouting powder in the ratio 10:2:1.  In a further container add water to some pva/white glue in the ratio of 1:10, for example, 1 teaspoon of pva to a small cupful of water.  Mix well together and add to the gravel grout and coat thoroughly.  Carefully press this mixture into the areas around the tesserae.

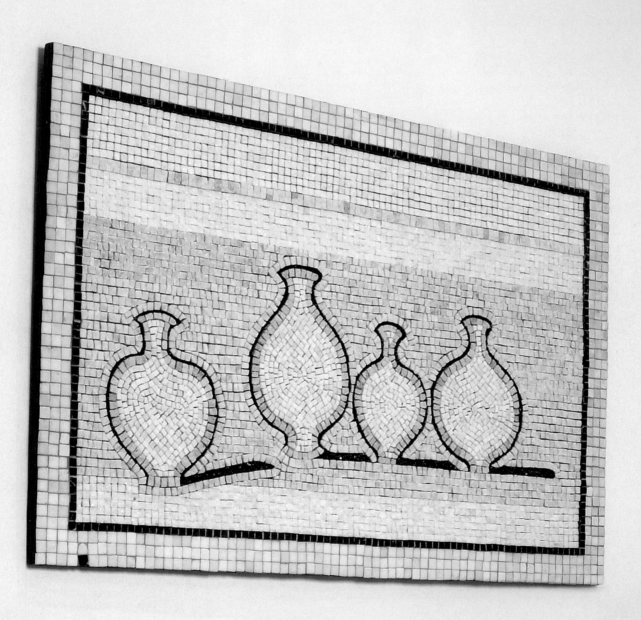

The completed work – *Classic Pots* – at home even in a very minimalist contemporary kitchen setting. Simplicity is a huge strength in the mosaic medium. Understanding this and utilizing it sensitively can lead to profound insights into the latent power in the art of mosaic making.

# Classic Pots

## The Inspirational Mosaic

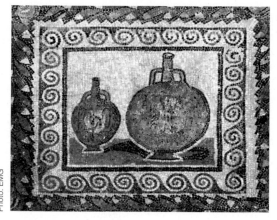

Photo: EMG

*Two pots, panel – detail from a Xenia[1] mosaic from El Jem, Bardo Museum, Tunis, Tunisia, 3rd century AD*

## Background Revelations

Nothing is much humbler than the simple pot or unguent bottle. This mosaic will celebrate it.

The Greeks and Romans created large quantities of pottery, complete remains of which, along with many hundreds of pottery shards, can be viewed in museums in cities and towns throughout the Mediterranean world.

Roman pottery was made on a wheel.

---

[1]The generic term *xenia* (Greek for 'hospitality') is given to the still life images of fruit, foodstuffs, and homely commodities often to be seen on a dining room floor in a *domus* or *villa*. Acknowledged as 'guests' presents', the owner could honor invitees and appear to proffer largesse.

The simplest types of pots or bottles were of unglazed earthenware fashioned from local clays into a form called *unguentaria*. These can be found in many sizes, the commonest ranging from about 2½in/6cm to 12in/30cm. They would have held a variety of ointments or oils, such as *cyprinum* (henna oil), jasmine and *nardinum* (spikenard), for use in the bathing process. Only the very wealthy would carry their precious oils to the baths/thermae in phials of gold, glass or alabaster.

Greek and Roman mosaics feature pottery as vases, vessels, bottles and amphorae (slender pots with a pointed base) in all their related functions, including domestic utility use, necessary drinking vessels in Dionysian revels, and as water, wine and oil containers.

They can also play a narrative role in ceremonial design or, as seen here, be used purely as images to give us decorative delight and largesse.

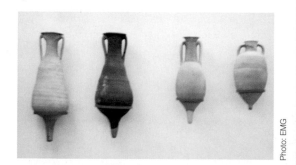

Photo: EMG

*Ancient Pots, Rabat Archaeological Museum, Morocco*

## Method

### The Drawing

Drawing the four pots and their shadows, carefully relating each pot to its neighbor.

### Equipment

Large sheet of white drawing paper,
  32in x 24in/80cm x 60cm
pencils
erasers
*Conté* crayon
ruler

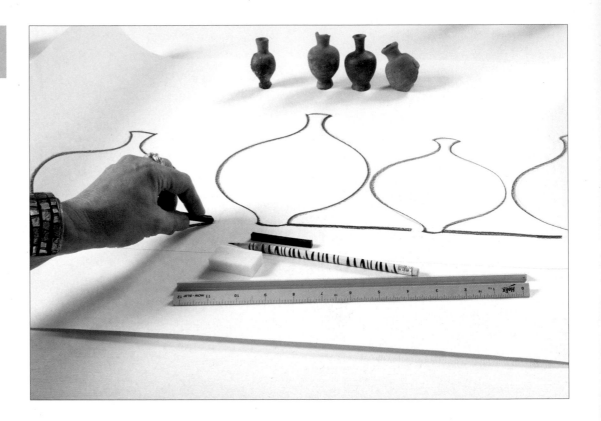

1 The drawing was done by eye, straight onto a large sheet of drawing paper. My aim was to create a design in which all four pots related to each other, evoking some kind of dialogue among themselves. Pots intrigue me. Often in an archaeological museum, when scrutinizing a mosaic, I am delighted to come upon a cabinet of pots displayed together – their rounded or elongated forms relate somehow to the human form and give off such an empathetic narration.

By adding shadow to each of the drawn pots, an extra dimension is given – one of implied substance – the pots immediately become holders of precious oils, water, honey or wine. Use the steel ruler or pencil to construct a wide border frame on all four sides.

When satisfied with the drawing, transfer it by eye to the large horizontally-laid rectangular backing timber. I have drawn a series of random parallel lines across the board, which will help later when laying the background in a simple *opus tessellatum*. Strengthen the pencil drawing with a wide overlay using the *conté* crayon. The thickness of the line will be an *aide-memoire* when constructing the vessels, as each will have an exterior surrounding grouting infill.

### Materials

½in/ 12mm exterior grade plywood 20in x 40in /
  60cm x 102cm
meter ruler
a palette of white marbles, including;
  ancient tesserae of *botticino* marble
  Carrara marble,
  *acquabianca* marble
  *biancone* marble
black *marquinia* marble.

---

**Secret Insight 1**

The little pots standing in the background and featured, much enlarged, in the drawing are some from an auction lot I was lucky enough to obtain at an antique sale. They are from Pompeii in Italy, and were therefore made before the eruption of Mount Vesuvius in 79 AD. They came from a present day house clearance; the ancestors of the family who lived there had in the 19th century been on the Grand Tour to Italy where, among other historical sites, they had visited Herculaneum and Pompeii and brought back the genuine articles!

## Concerning the Cutting Technique

Cutting marble – *biancone* – on the hardie, with a mosaic hammer. This mosaic will be made throughout with various naturally occurring white marbles.

The most exact cutting of marble, a natural stone with a variable nature, is on the hardie, using a hammer. This tried and tested technique is worth persevering with when first encountering what may seem like a lethal tool. Do not be alarmed. Keep in mind the following pointers:

- good posture; sit at a comfortable height to the hardie (a chisel ended tool generally embedded in a trunk of wood) to allow for a good downward action with the hammer in the cutting hand.

- gently grip the trunk of the tree firmly with your knees to keep it steady (mine has a tendency to wobble).
- give careful consideration in placing the tessera to be cut. It should nearly always be cut in half (and then again and again etc) – so accurate placing on the chisel-edge is paramount.
- raise the cutting hand with the hammer held well up the handle and swing it down directly onto the tessera so that it lines up with the hardie.

This is it – practice – and be in control (nervous hesitations are a no no!); good considered positioning of the tesserae, and swift and accurate cuttings, result in wonderful cleanly cut tesserae, time after time…

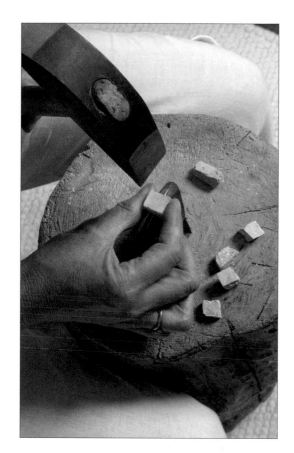

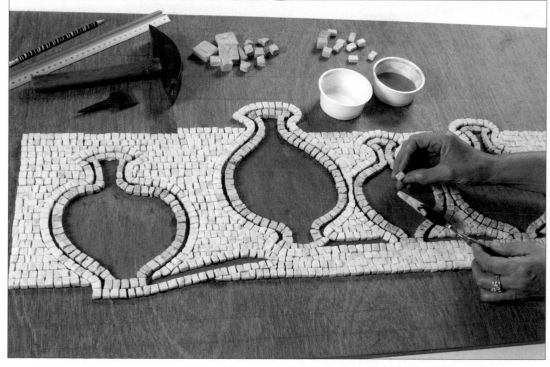

2 Putting adhesive onto the back of the tesserae to build up the background in horizontal rows of white, largely cube-shaped tesserae, *opus tessellatum*.

After outlining the pots with the ancient marble tesserae, the first background tesserae of *acquabianco* marble were laid to follow the contours of the vessels but leaving a generous gap for a textural grout. A gap was also left under each pot for a textural grout shadow. The lines of *opus tessellatum* then immediately followed, each stopping short of the surrounding wide border.

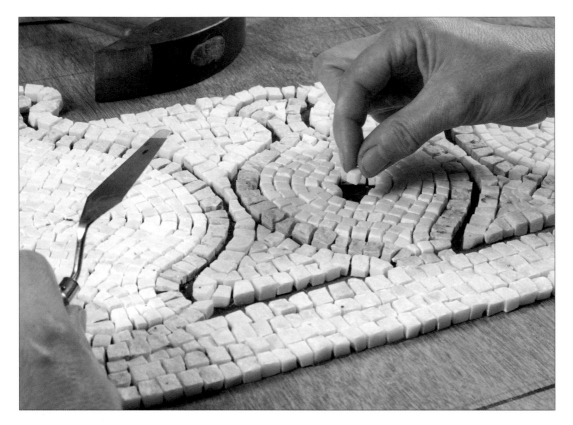

3  Before continuing too far and to give time to contemplate other background possibilities, the little pots were filled in using small tesserae of Carrara marble, some with more impurities of color than usual; such are the vagaries of a natural stone. I contoured the inner edge of the pot and continued filling in to the center. The use of a smaller dimension of tesserae gives special visual emphasis to the pot forms, and also allows a more exacting articulation of the pot shape.

**Secret Insight 2**

Many years ago I was given a bag of ancient *botticino* marble tesserae (I believe they came from a site in ancient Tlemçen in Algeria). It is these I have finally used in the contouring of the pots. Many still have a Roman lime mortar attached to the sides of the tesserae.

4  Continue building up the background. Firm up the border frame with a ruler-drawn line, using a felt tipped pen. The *opus tessellatum* background continues to fill up the space, stopping at the edges of the frame. In order to add subtle interest into the background I have used different marbles from time to time and slightly differing sizes. This introduces a richer texture into such a large area, and the oblique variations of color, size and texture will allow the beauty intrinsic in the materials to be appreciated.

The mosaic will be edged with a very simple retaining frame, in cubes of white and black marble. The black is laid nearest the image, to frame the image visually, and the three rows of white marble are laid to the outer edge to give a sense of the infinite, or the uncontained – their white color leading the eye into space. This will be very effective when hung on a white wall.

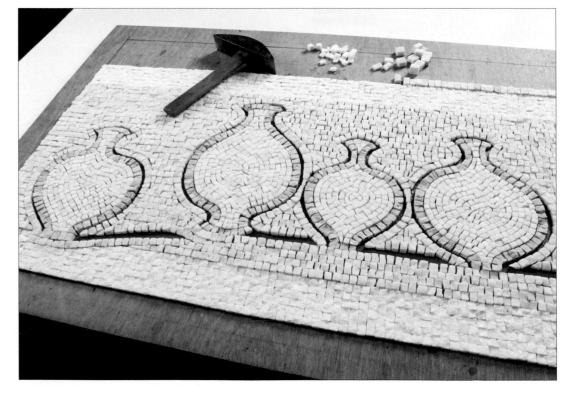

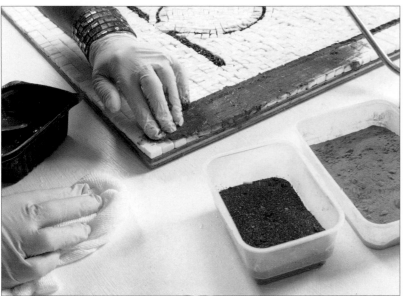

## Grouting and infill

## Materials

For the *Grouting*:
Portland cement
sand (in this case from Trevignano
    Romano on the banks of Lago di
    Bracciano, Italy)
water
containers
small trowel
cloths
protective gloves

For the *Infill*:
pva adhesive/white glue
glass chippings (frit)
lava from Mount Vesuvius (lava del
    Vesuvio) (optional)
flat palette knife
containers
prodder
a proprietary silicon sealer
container

5 Grouting the simple border of cut cubes of black *marquinia* marble and white Carrara marble. In this work, the border frame alone is grouted. The grout was made with sand and cement in a ratio of 4:1. (The sand is dark and volcanic and links the mosaic again with the area around Pompeii.) Mix the sand and cement together using the trowel, and slowly add the water to form a good thickish mix. Wear the gloves and rub the mix carefully into the frame, being sure to fill all the interstices between the tesserae. Clean with cloths, and cover with a damp cloth for up to three days for the very slow, strong hardening process to occur. Clean the surface with water and when dry seal the edges of the mosaic with a proprietary sealer of a black color, using a flat palette knife. Allow one edge to dry first, before proceeding to another.

6 Adding the glass 'frit' infill to the crevice around the pots. The areas around the pots are filled with glass frit and the shadows are filled with Vesuvian lava, resplendent with the wondrous colors of fused silicon, which occurred from the time of the eruption of Mount Vesuvius. This small amount of Vesuvian lava was bought from a souvenir vendor when I was visiting the area some years ago.

    Both the frit and the lava are added individually to a mix of water and pva adhesive or white glue and carefully pressed into the areas around the pots and shadows respectively. Allow the infills to dry overnight, keeping the mosaic flat. The adhesive/water mix will dry colorless and hold the textural glassy grouts in place, adding rich dark color and intrigue.

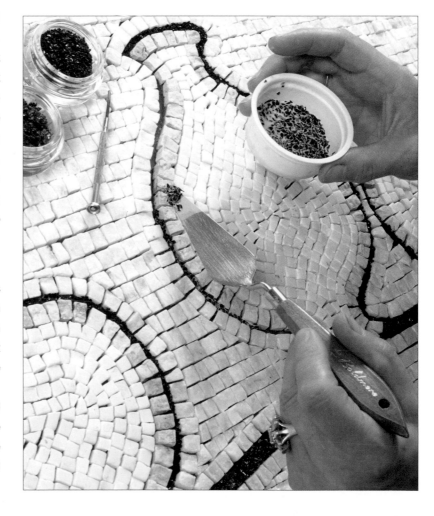

# 3D Spiral Frieze

## The Inspirational Mosaic

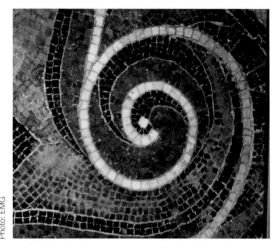

Photo: EMG

*Three dimensional scroll pattern, detail, 1st century BCE. Museum of Roman Antiquities, Rabat, Malta*

## Background Revelations

The mosaic floors of the Rabat Museum in Malta are from a Roman *domus* or town house and are a visual treat. Each room features a mosaic with a wide polychrome border of marvelous optical effect. Two floors have meanders of remarkable complexity and illusionistic depth and another has a central *emblema*, or inserted mosaic, with an image of nymphs punishing a satyr. The border to this mosaic has a unique and memorable three-dimensional spiral design which extends on all four sides. This is my inspiration.

*Emblema* (pl. *emblemata*) – these are panels which, after making, are inserted into a

floor mosaic. In the classical era they were composed on a separate matrix of stone, terracotta or marble, and made away from site in an *officina*, with tremendous skill and dexterity, often using very small tesserae.

The *officina* (pl. *officinae*) – these are mosaic workshops, and occur frequently throughout the Mediterranean and beyond. Some of the greatest centers of excellence in the early Hellenic tradition of mosaic making, of which the image on the right is a fine example, are also to be found at Pergamon (Turkey, Asia Minor); Antioch (Antakya/Hatay, South East Anatolia, Turkey); and Alexandria (Egypt).

The designs created may well have derived from pattern books featuring various figurative designs and geometric and floral motifs, and would be chosen by the commissioning villa or *domus* owner.

Both the spiral and the meander have a long history, appearing on pottery in the 6th millennium BCE. The spiral in particular can be found in many historical sites on the island of Malta, on its notable 3rd millennium BCE stone monuments. An example is at Tarzien, where the stone screens and altars of the 4th and 3rd millennium BCE temples are uniquely decorated with geometric patterns, giving a special emphasis to the spiral.

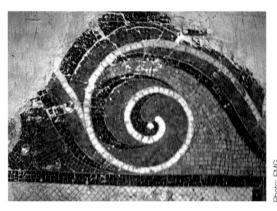

Photo: EMG

*Detail, three-dimensional scroll motif, 1st century BCE, Rabat, Malta*

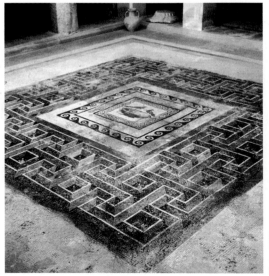

*A further room of the domus, showing a wide polychrome framing meander pattern, with superb three-dimensional effects*

Photo: EMG

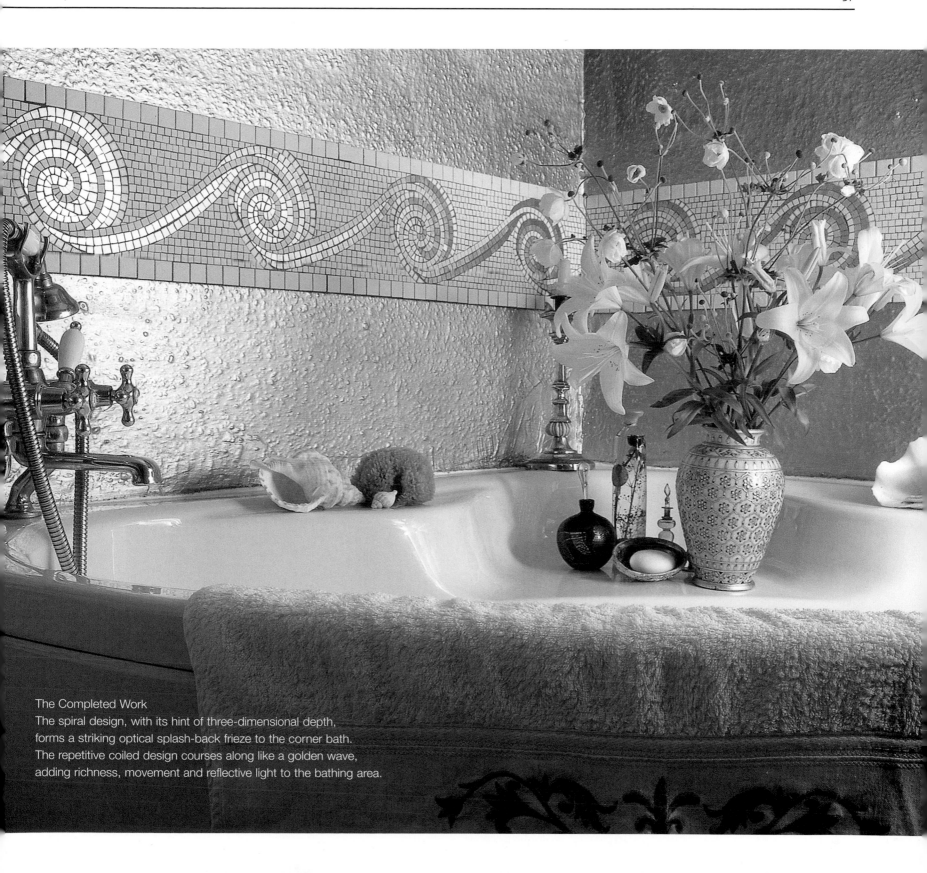

The Completed Work
The spiral design, with its hint of three-dimensional depth,
forms a striking optical splash-back frieze to the corner bath.
The repetitive coiled design courses along like a golden wave,
adding richness, movement and reflective light to the bathing area.

## Method

### The Drawing

Building up a drawing of continuous spirals along the lengths of timber, using a variety of inks to differentiate various sections.

### Equipment

Two varying lengths of ½ in/ 12mm marine plywood, 72in x 9in / 163cm x 23cm, and 91in x 9in/ 231cm x 23cm (each measured to fit alongside a corner bath)

ruler

pencils

eraser

golds, white and black inks

brushes

### Concerning the Backing Board

When in doubt about which plywood to use in mosaic, tend towards exterior plywood. However, where any possible humid or damp situations are incurred for the mosaic, choose a marine ply as a backing timber. The resins used to bond the wood in this case are water-resistant and less susceptible to wet conditions. Wood of any kind can never be one hundred percent damp-proofed. With plywood, the cut edge is the most vulnerable part and should invariably be sealed with a water-resistant sealer or protected by a frame.

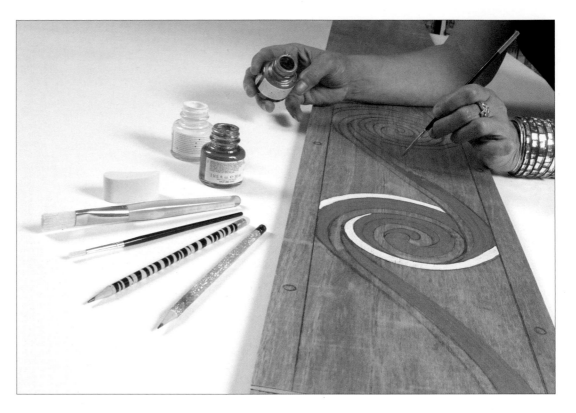

1 On each length of timber draw two narrow parallel lines to indicate a border a whole tesserae width, 1in x 1in/25mm x 25mm. Within the remaining area a three dimensional running scroll frieze will be drawn. Determine the length of each scroll and its position in the design. The spiraling motif can be as simple or as complex as you wish. I wanted just to hint at an optical depth for each spiral, enough to engage the bather in an optical intrigue while relaxing in the bath.

Repeat the pencil drawing along the length of the two timber panels by re-tracing each spiral and tail, or continue with the drawing by eye.

To help with the construction of the mosaic, use the colored inks to indicate which colors are to be used and where. Finally, mark areas at regular intervals along the border which are to be drilled as fixing holes when the mosaic is placed in position.

### Materials

white ceramic tiles, 1in x 1in/25mm x 25mm and ¾in x ¾in / 20mm x 20mm

vitreous glass tiles ¾in x ¾in/ 20mm x 20mm

three shades of Venetian gold leaf glass cut into tesserae of approximately ⅜in x ⅜in / 10mm x 10mm

wheeled hand nippers (for the glass)

standard hand nippers (for the ceramic)

pva/white glue

container

palette knife

2 Placing the cut golden tesserae. Use the two darkest shades of gold to begin the constructing of the spirals. Generally the shapes of the tesserae will be square, but from time to time triangular forms are needed in the design where the linear spirals converge.

Each spiral – twelve in all – is constructed in the same way. It is easier and more fulfilling in the long run to do all the work of one color throughout the frieze, rather than complete each individual spiral – this more 'fluid' procedure is one to remember when working on lengthy repetitive motifs.

The white vitreous glass tesserae and the matt white ceramic tesserae help define each spiral. Their reflective and absorbing surfaces respectively give illusions of depth and surface value. The palest gold will be used in the central area of each spiral.

Lay the border in larger uncut ceramic tiles before filling in the inner remaining area with horizontal lines of square-shaped tesserae, which will form a stabilizing background for the spiral design.

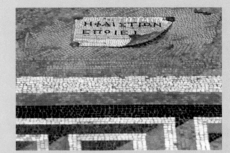

**Secret Insight 1**

In this example of a 3D meander made in the Hellenic period and of tiny tesserae, there remains no central emblema but something else is saved – the signature of Hephaeston, one of the greatest of Greek mosaic artists. The signature appears as if on parchment, curved at the bottom right in a brilliant feat of mosaic *trompe l'oeil*. It reads "Hephaeston did it", to draw attention to his name and prowess. 2nd century BCE, from the Palace of the Acropolis, Pergamon (Bergama), Turkey; Pergamon Museum, Berlin, Germany.

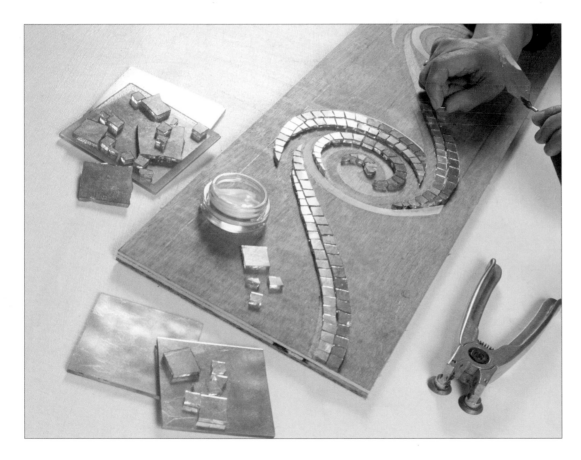

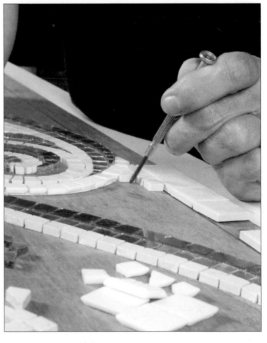

3 Using the prodder to place a triangular tessera in position where the background meets the spiral form. Acutely angled or triangular-shaped tesserae will need to be cut whenever the background design meets the spiral at an angle. This shape is most easily produced by cutting a tile in half to give two rectangles, and then angling the triangular cutting edge of the mosaic nipper to cut quite acutely across the rectangular half of tile. Cut with a firm action. Triangular shapes are not the easiest shape to cut – do not despair.

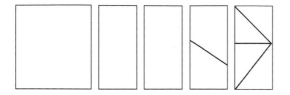

To cut acutely angled or triangular-shaped tesserae shapes first cut a tile in half to give two rectangles, and then angle the triangular cutting edge of the mosaic nipper to cut quite acutely across the rectangular half of tile. Always cut with a firm action. Triangular shapes are not the easiest shape to cut, but practice makes perfect.

# Grouting

## Materials

a proprietary ready-mixed fine gray grout

plastic containers

water

gloves

trowel

cloths

mortar cleaner (a brand containing HCL – hydrochloric acid)

brushes

protective gloves

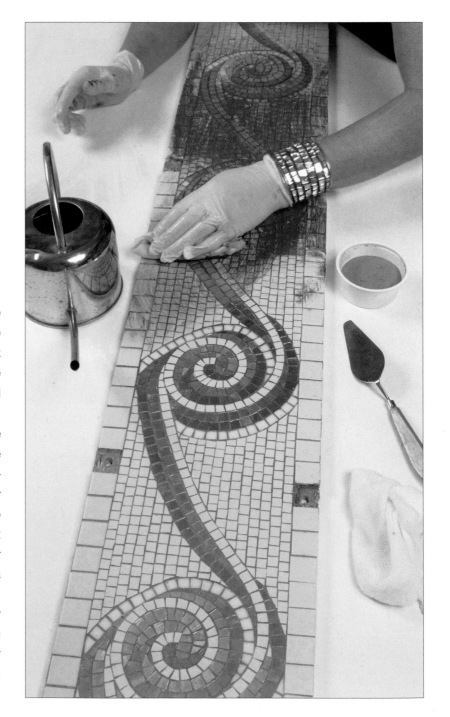

4 Put an amount, about three cupfuls, of the proprietary grout in the container and use the trowel to mix with the water, which should be added cautiously as a fairly stiff grouting mortar is required – too runny a mix may warp the backing timber by seeping into the wood, or alternatively cause areas of uneven grouting and little sunken craters, and result in a weakened and uneven mortar.

Wearing gloves, rub this grout mix over all the surface of the mosaic, filling all the gaps and taking care at the edges. Wipe the surface clean, and leave under a dampened cloth for the curing process to develop – about three days. Wash the mosaic surface with clean water until it is clear of cement. Sometimes a little mortar cleaner containing acid may be used to clear away any cement residue left on the tiles, particularly the absorbent ceramic tiles. In this case, an open-air clean up is advised, and great care for safety observed. Wear protective gloves and add a little of the cleaner to a container of water, or use undiluted and carefully brush over the surface, being careful not to splash the acid at any time. The cement is immediately acted upon, and the mosaic can be washed down straight after application with large amounts of water. Leave the areas to dry naturally and again lay the friezes down flat to stop any warping – timber is very sensitive to misuse.

## Hanging

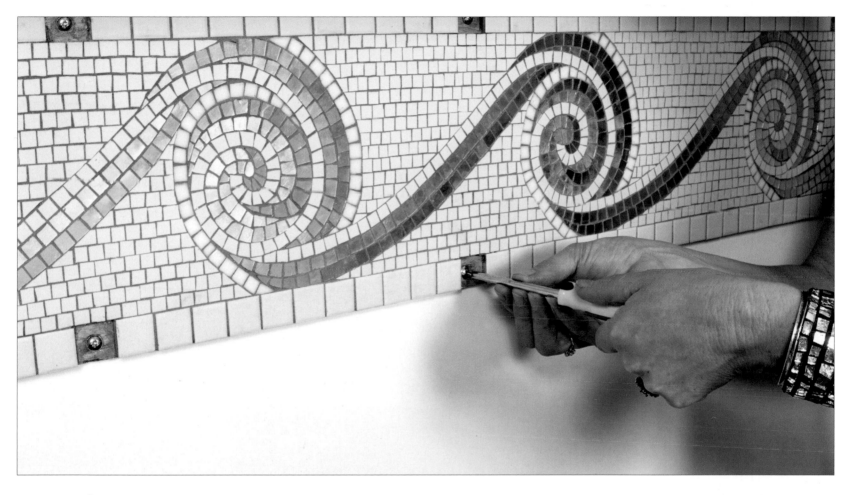

## Materials

electric drill

plastic screw anchors
   (Rawlplugs or Tapits)

screws

screw driver

additional border tiles

adhesive

palette knife

additional grout mix

cloths

5 Screwing the frieze in position on the bathroom wall. The two spiral friezes will be sited above each side of a corner bath. Determine their position and drill the wall accordingly. Gently hammer the plastic screw anchors into the drilled holes and using the screws, begin to hang the friezes, securing the upper central area first. When all the screws are in position, adhere an uncut border tile over each screw head. Prepare a little of the ready-mixed grout to grout in each "camouflage" tile. Clean. The area may be slightly raised (because of the head of the screw). This will pinpoint where to uncover if at any time the work is to be dismantled. You may wish to disguise this feature for a more permanent siting by countersinking each screw into the timber, before adding the single border tiles and grouting.

# Golden Spiral Dining Table

## The Inspirational Mosaic

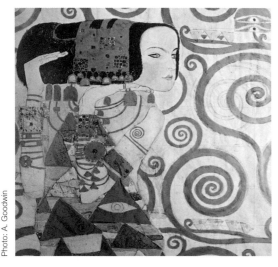

*Expectancy by Gustav Klimt, detail from the cartoon for the drawing room frieze for the Stoclet House, Brussels, Belgium, 1905*

## Background Revelations

This close up detail comes from an iconic work, known and loved by many an artist and art-lover alike. In its 100 years of existence, it has influenced those who work with textiles, artworks and mosaics.[1]

Gustav Klimt (1862-1918) was an artist of unique significance, with a distinct idiosyncratic style and works of great decorative clarity. Born in Vienna, the capital of Austria, he was a founder member (1897) of the Viennese Secession, a group of like-minded artists whose intentions were to raise the flagging Austrian art scene up to international standards. Later, in 1906, Klimt was to be made president of the Austrian Art Institute. From 1903 Klimt became an active member of a group called the *Wiener Werkstätte*, through which he explored close links between textile patterning and jewelry, and various other decorative media. "Applied arts," he enthused, was "art applied to life." Under Klimt's guidance, it was this group that in 1909 began work on the mosaics for the town home in Brussels of the businessman Adolphe Stoclet, a dwelling designed by Klimt's great friend, the Moravian-born architect Josef Hoffman (1870-1956), and a building in itself a poetic masterpiece.

Son of Ernst Klimt, a gold engraver, Klimt had, from early 1885, introduced gold paint into his work, a material which was to have added significance after his visit in 1903 to Ravenna, Italy, where he viewed the early Byzantine mosaics resplendent with gold-leaf glass.

Klimt's style, which always gave strong emphasis to the contours of an image, had found a sympathetic métier in mosaic, a medium delighting in the ornamental and the luscious.

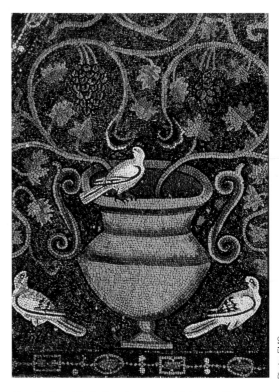

*Detail, San Vitale Presbytery, mid-6th c. AD, Ravenna, showing golden vine spirals on a rich indigo blue ground*

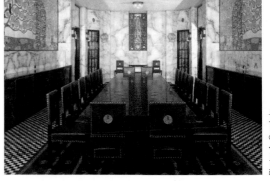

[1]The esteemed School of Mosaic at Spilimbergo, Friuli, Italy, frequently encourages its pupils, by facsimile making, to study the works of Gustav Klimt.

*Right: Dining room of the Palais Stoclet, Brussels, showing the "mosaic frieze" by Gustav Klimt, 1906-11*

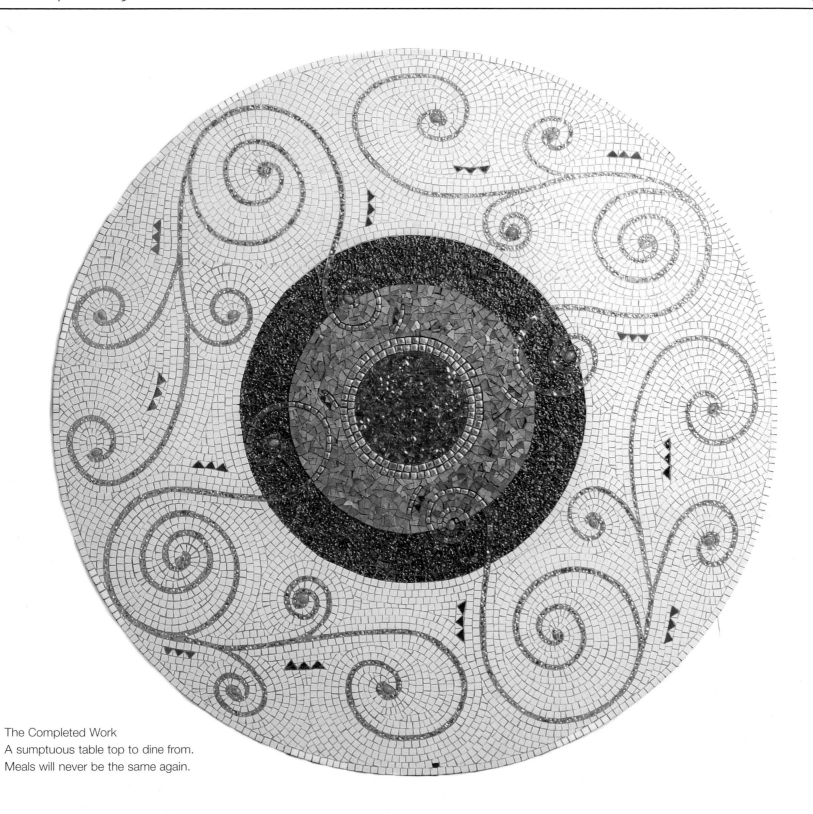

The Completed Work
A sumptuous table top to dine from.
Meals will never be the same again.

## Method

### The Drawing

The drawing was made directly onto a circular exterior plywood base. The spirals highlighted are in gold inks, and the inner concentric areas in rich acrylic color.

### Equipment

½in/12mm exterior plywood, from which a circle
    was cut, 41in/144cm in diameter
360° protractor
large format compass
small compass
pencils
eraser
gold felt-tipped pens
brushes
gold inks
turquoise and blue metallic paints

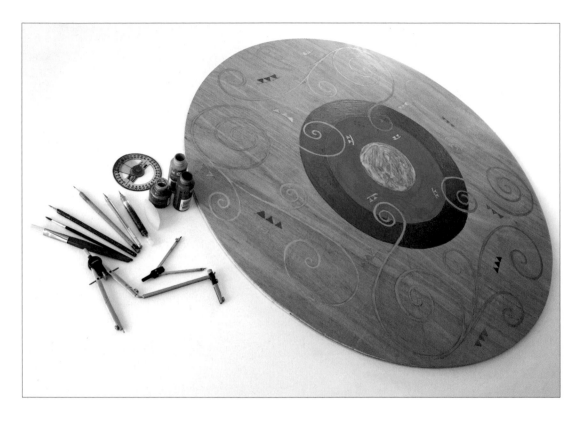

1 Large concentric circles were drawn with the compasses at intervals on the timber backing board. A border was provided wide enough to take a ¾in/20mm tessera cut into four. The protractor was used to find the four cardinal points, to divide the circular panel into four equally-sized sections.

As the spirals were randomly drawn in pencil, careful attention was given to the area sections to ensure a certain design balance for the whole design. When satisfied with the design, the linear spiral forms, which should cover an area large enough to support a dining plate, were outlined with gold pens and ink.

Some further design shapes were added, inspired by the Klimt drawing. In this case, the equilateral triangular forms in groups of three (for the outer area) and two (for the inner section) in colors of gold and sapphire blue appealed. Finally the inner concentric frieze areas were shaded in with dominant colors, turquoise, sapphire blue, and gold. At least one of these areas will be richly textured.

## Materials

Venetian gold-leaf (smooth and rippled)
Ravenna mirror glass
stained glass
ornamental scarabs (beetle-shaped ceramic
    ornaments with a turquoise-colored glaze)
golden glass cubes
lightly glazed ceramic tiles
unglazed ceramic tiles
turquoise oval-shaped ornaments
wheeled mosaic nippers
standard nippers
white glue/pva adhesive
black ink
brushes
black powder pigment
palette knife

## Concerning the Laying Techniques

The method used throughout will be that commonly known as the "direct technique" – that is, the tesserae will be fixed to the backing timber, the surface always uppermost. This, for me, is the most satisfying of all techniques used in mosaic, as at all times the mosaicist has a direct visual rapport with the work – what is put down is what is seen, a true involvement.

In this design, two direct techniques will be explored. One is a simple laying of tesserae using a pva glue or white glue, piece by piece. In the other, each tessera will be pressed into a thickened adhesive. In the first instance the area produced will be flat, and in the latter, a varied textural surface will result.

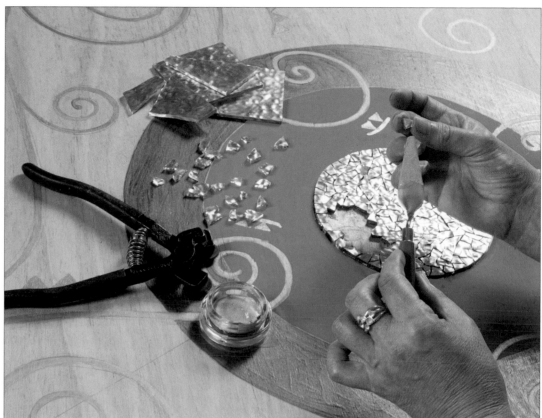

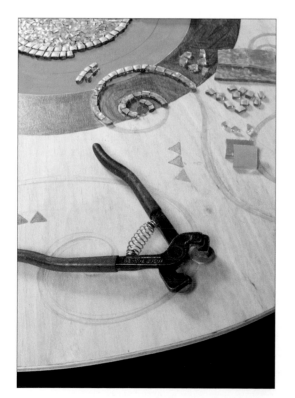

2 The tesserae are cut, and fixed with a white glue/pva with added black ink to make a dark gray setting adhesive.

Begin work on the central inner circle using cubes of gold to transcribe the circle. When placing the cut tesserae for the infill, use the straight edge of the granulated Venetian gold to contour a good edge, and then proceed to fill the circle in, using a crazy paving technique now popularly known as *opus palladianum*

3 Begin to outline the spirals in tesserae of rectangular shape.Use the golden tesserae cut into narrow rectangular "running lines" to draw the spirals. Vary the texture of each in each section, e.g., use the smoothest gold in the turquoise section, the gently rippled gold in the blue section, and the granulated gold for the large outer section.  Add the grouped triangles using a further surface gold color. Also add the oval-shaped ornaments

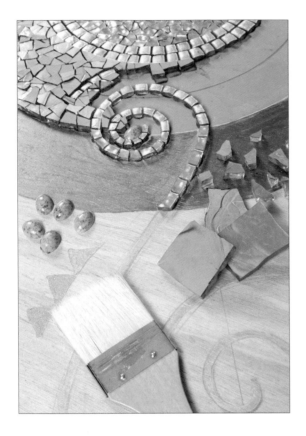

**4** Fill in one area with richly-colored handmade turquoise gold. Use the turquoise gold, which has a distinctive surface color variation and is of variable thickness, to build up an area of strong textural interest. The turquoise tesserae are glued to the base using the adhesive with added black powder pigment; this thickens the glue, its texture allowing very slight angling of the tesserae.

It may seem inappropriate to have a dining table with a gently uneven inner area of color and materials, but I wanted to emphasize that the lusciousness of the materials can complement the sensory experience of eating – adding a visual enjoyment to any subsequent mouth-watering ones.

Place either oval ornaments or ornamental scarabs at the focal points of each spiral. These give strong and textural starting points to each spiral as it unravels in expanding curves. The little ornamental beetles (scarabs are symbolic of life – rising out of the earth or dung at sunrise and returning at sundown), alongside other decorative elements, add an exotic Egyptian-izing air to the design. This great and ancient civilization initiated many of the items in our accepted encyclopedia of ornamental motifs and played an important inspirational role in Klimt's life.

The last of the three inner circles of rich color is created by inverting the Venetian granulated gold to show the metal glowing through its turquoise backing glass. Again, add powder pigment to the adhesive to form a thick setting medium. In this case, the thicker quality of the glue will also help even out any excessive granulation in the material and allow it to adhere more evenly to the backing timber.

Continue forming the spirals in lines of rectangular tesserae, ending each curve with the little scarab ornaments.

**5** Use the standard nippers to cut a ceramic edge. It is advisable to apply a simple edging of tesserae at this point so that the spirals are formed well within the border edge. White glazed and unglazed tiles are cut into four for this procedure. This simple varying of the surface of the same color of material continues the richly textural theme of the design.

Add the small decorative triangles to the design in colors of deep turquoise and rich gold in groups of three – echoing the Klimt design with its Egyptian overtones.

All the remaining area will be filled using unglazed ceramic tiles cut into four and built up using *opus vermiculatum*. This is a lovely flowing opus, most specially effective where a series of curves occur, as wonderful movement is evoked within the placing of the tesserae, giving rise to the term *andamento* – a flowing or coursing occurrence in the medium, so appealing with its metaphysical overtones, and often underlying an organic basis to a design; e.g., an ideal background for laying tesserae in mosaics with a revelatory or horticultural content.

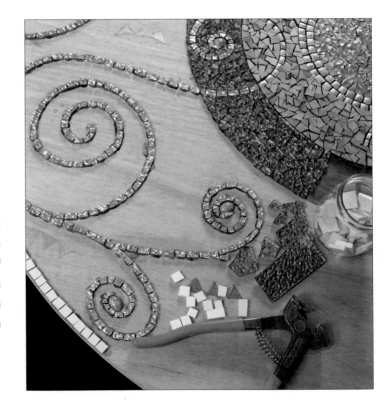

6 Building up the background in *opus vermiculatum*, using white unglazed ceramic tiles.

Use the standard nippers to cut the white, unglazed ceramic tesserae into four. Each quarter tessera can be laid in position using adhesive without added pigment. Outline all the spirals with at least an initial row of tesserae, before building up the background. When undecided about which way to lay the tesserae next, choose directions which give greatest emphasis to the spiraling movement. When all the outer area has been filled, allow to dry thoroughly before the grouting procedure begins.

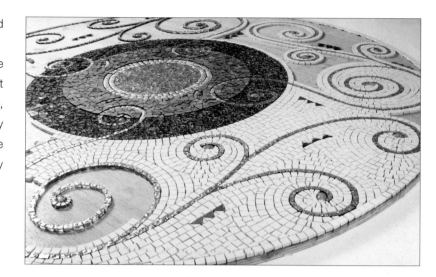

## Grouting

## Materials

| | | |
|---|---|---|
| a proprietary ready-mixed | trowel | silicon buffing cloth |
|   fine gray grout | cloths | |
| plastic containers | mortar cleaner | |
| protective gloves | water | |

7 Wearing protective gloves, mix a quantity of ready-mixed grout – about 6 cups – by adding water carefully to form a stiffish mortar. Proceed to rub this into the whole mosaic, taking special care over the textural area. Take time over difficult areas, for example, around the decorative scarab ornaments, and at any irregular surface heights. Grouting should be an enjoyable process, as it reveals a true characteristic of mosaic. Allow plenty of time for the procedure, being sure to grout thoroughly.

Using the cloths, clean off excess grout with great care, and allow the work to dry under dampened cloths for up to three days. The scum that will then be seen on the surface can be washed away with a light hosing of water or very gentle brushing down with water. Use plenty of clean water in the surface cleaning procedure.

Allow the mosaic to dry naturally, before using the silicon buffing cloth; a glass or mirror cleaning cloth could also be used to buff up the glazed inner area of the work for maximum light reflection.

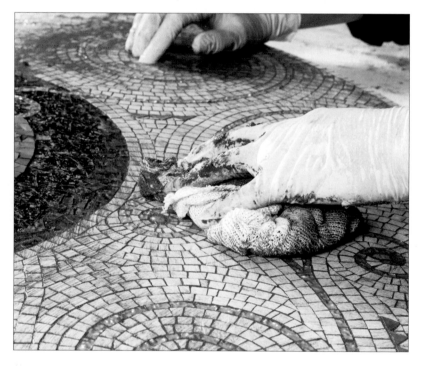

## The Framing

The mosaic can be edged or framed in a variety of ways, for example, using a simple ceramic mosaic tile surround, or a waterproof sealer. A more elaborate metal frame could be made – or the work mounted onto an existing table base. Whichever way is chosen to "set off" the mosaic, be sure that the framing materials used complement the golden spiral design as a whole, to ensure a complete ensemble.

# Exteriors and Gardens

## Historical Viewpoints

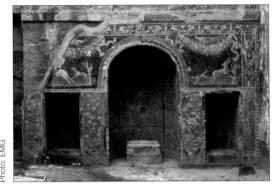

Photo: EMG

*The courtyard showing the arched* nymphaeum *with shell-decorated side niches,* House of Neptune and Amphitrite, *1st century AD, Herculaneum, Italy*

The fountains and *nymphaea* (watery grottoes where the mythological nymphs played) of Herculaneum and Pompeii herald a beginning for external and garden mosaics.

The exterior setting seemed to unleash the mind and introduce imaginative juxtapositioning of surfaces, materials and imagery. The small mosaic-decorated rear courtyard of the House of Poseidon (Roman: Neptune; Greek: Poseidon), God of the Seas and his consort Salacia (Roman: Amphitrite) is resplendent with light and color. The mosaics are bordered by real shells, most probably locally sourced as Herculaneum in the first century was a seaside town.[1]

The fountains created in early Roman times had irregular surfaces, and incorporated a variety of miscellaneous objects, such as stone and shells as well as glass. This latter often reflected both light and the movement of water – phenomena exaggerated by being externalized and at the mercy of the sun and weather.

The private garden has become for many artists working today, a place where they can create a fantastical world combining ideas with materials in uniquely personal ways. For the

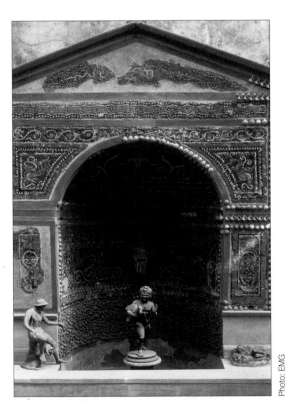

Photo: EMG

Nymphaeum, *from the House of the Scientists / Casa degli Scienziati, 1st century AD, Pompeii, Italy; showing glass (blue frit), cockle shells (cardium edule) and white shells (murex brandarie)*

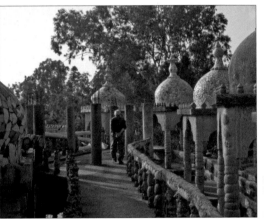

Photo: EMG

*The Rock Garden, detail, 2000, by Nek Chand Saini (seen in the photograph above), Chandigarh, India, showing recent architectural forms decorated with discarded china*

following artists, their private passions have become public sites, open to curious visitors.

Sometimes an initially small and secluded garden can grow out of all proportion – as can be seen in the Rock Garden, Chandigarh, India (begun 1952), the work of the Indian artist Nek Chand Saini – an untutored master of mosaic making. He was born in Sialkot district (Pakistan)

[1]Herculaneum, like neighboring Pompeii and Stabiae, in Campania in Southern Italy, was buried under volcanic ash by the eruption of Mount Vesuvius on the morning of 24 August 79 AD. Only in the mid-19th century was a systematic excavation undertaken – yet to date barely a quarter of the town has been excavated. The principal finds are to be seen in the National Archaeological Museum of Naples, Italy.

in 1924 and moved to India in 1947 where he became an inspector of roads. Nek Chand's initial creations were contained in a secretly hidden space of public land near the Sukhna Lake.[2]

Conceived as a kingdom, the garden grew out of the fantastical vision of a simply-born man. It was initially constructed from a wide variety of waste materials, e.g., broken porcelain sanitary ware, electric bulbs, bangles, discarded glass ware, and found stones, each transformed into precious constructing materials.

The garden was officially opened to the public in 1976 – but work continues by Nek

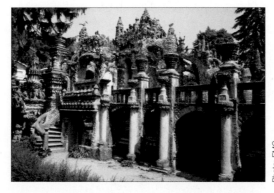

[2]The town of Chandigarh, India; plan of the site, 1950: the red X indicates the site of the Rock Garden.

The city of Chandigarh where Nek Chand Saini developed his organic creation, the Rock Garden, was also an artistic creation, but ironically one of extreme logic and heightened rationale. It was designed by the Swiss-born artist/architect Charles Edouard Jeanneret – known as Le Corbusier (1887-1965). This capital city of the Punjab region is built as a grid, with zoning dividing the city into many sectors. Yet for all its strict formality, it is high in the affection of the city's residents

Chand to the present day, as a park with swings and open gathering areas have been added this century. It is a spell-binding garden, peopled with animals, figures, waterfalls, theatre and landscaped walkways and palaces. It is vast, over 30 hectares / 75 acres, and attracts thousands of visitors.

Yet Nek Chand has never considered himself an artist, but accepts the term with a smile. It is truly a visionary place and an outstanding example of what can be achieved when the mosaic medium is in the hands of an instinctive master of creativity.

France has been the homeland of a variety of instinctive creators. Perhaps the earliest known was Facteur Cheval (1836-1924), a postman by profession working in Hauterives in the Drôme region of Southern France. He too, out of an untutored imagination, created an extraordinary exterior garden monument known as the Palais Ideal. It is built of stones assembled in a mosaic-like manner, where a host of birds and angels embellish a composite architectural fantasy containing aspects of a mosque, Hindu temple, feudal castle, Khmer sanctuary, and even a Swiss chalet. Cheval, too, never claimed to be a sculptor or an architect, but he is an acknowledged

The Palais Ideal, *detail, the east face (1879-1912), by Facteur Cheval, Hauterives, France*

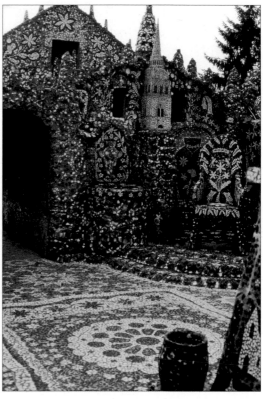

Picassiette, *detail, the Black courtyard and throne (1938-1962), by Raymond Isidore, Chartres, France*

solitary visionary who, through imagination and determination, created a wonder of art.

Other untutored artists in France, working from inner conviction, include the acknowledged supremist Raymond Isidore (1900-1964) from Chartres, who created a home and garden of intense devotional application out of shards and fragments of glass, china and miscellaneous fragments.

It was while he was working as a cemetery caretaker in his beloved city of Chartres that he was transfixed by a glinting shard of glass on one of his walks, which led to his obsession with construction through fragments of china and crockery. Around 1938 he began work decorating the interior of his home with china and tile. He covered everything – sewing machine, bed, chairs, cooker – all that could be, was given a mosaic veneer. A deeply religious man he continued his devotions to both his new creative drive and his religion, in the decorating of his small house. Of his creative energy he is quoted as saying "I followed my spirit in the same way as one follows a path."

He was nicknamed Picassiette, ironically called the Picasso of plates or "plate stealer". Now, after his death, his home and garden are affectionately called 'Picassiette' and have become regarded as one of the compulsory tourist attractions to be seen by visitors and devotees to the great pilgrimage city of Chartres.

Other artists working in France who followed their dream with a devoted passion are Euclides Ferreira da Costa (1902-1989) from Vilarinho in Portugal, who lived in Dives-sur-Mer, and the contemporary artist Renée Bodin (b. 1927), known as Hurfane, who originally came

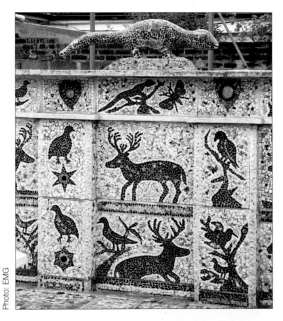

Photo: EMG

La Maison Bleue, *detail, a wall of animals, crowned with a 3D reptile, by Euclides Ferreira da Costa*

from Algeria and who now lives outside Chartres at Happonvilliers.

Ferrera da Costa came to Dives sur Mer in 1924 and began work on his home and garden in 1957. His work, which covers 300 square meters / c. 350 square yards, features animals, reptiles and birds, remembered and recorded. Much of the work is made of glass, plates, and tile, heavily grouted in richly pigmented blue cement – hence the name of his work, "La Maison Bleue". There is again a devotional aspect to the work, as places of pilgrimage are constructed and embellished, e.g., Lourdes cathedral in France, and the cathedral of Our Lady of Fatima in Portugal.

The work unfolds with a quiet intimacy as one construction follows another in a closely confined space. Sadly the work of this impassioned creator is in a state of neglect today. Like the work of the featured artist, Simon Rodia, it is hoped that dedicated admirers will reinstate the work as a national monument, and an association to this effect inaugurated in 2004.[3]

Renée Bodin's passion is a dream of delights and unraveling. Her work, Les Jardins de la Feuilleraie (begun 1980) is divided into two sections – le Jardin Rose, and le Jardin Bleu. They narrate the life of this gentle yet passionate artist in manufactured glass, unusual for an exterior work of size. The work depicts many idiosyncratic events and moments as well as household pets – her beloved cats are touchingly rendered and remembered as part of her reverie.

From time to time artists reach outside the intimately known world. In the work of the

---

[3] An association was established recently to save la Maison Bleue for posterity, and the French Heritage Foundation is now involved with the restoration project: for details see the website at http://www.dives-sur-mer.com/index.php?var=mb and links.

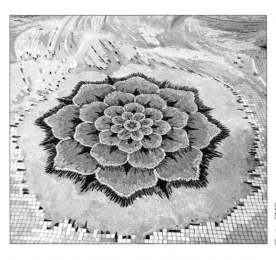

Photo: EMG

Les Jardins de la Feuilleraie, *detail, le Jardin Bleu, by Renée Bodin, Happonvilliers, Chartres, France*

artist Niki de Sainte Phalle (1930-2002) the occult is involved in her personal journey. Although born in France she was educated in New York, but a trip to Barcelona in Spain to see the works of Antoni Gaudì in 1955 changed her life and influenced her vision.

In 1979 she began work on a hillside at Garavicchio in southern Tuscany, Italy, on what is considered to be her major work: Il Giardino dei Tarochi – the Tarot Garden.

For Niki her garden project symbolized life, played out as a game of cards in which the rules are learned as life is experienced. The ancient Tarot philosophy of mystery and magic is interpreted in symbolic sculptures – the 22 major Arcana of the Tarot. These are exhibited as mosaic-encrusted forms in a natural setting, divided by pathways on which texts and poems are written.

Each of the artist's pictorial representations was made in tandem with her own life experience, its joys and its downfalls. Whilst working on the garden, Niki lived alone inside one of her sculptures, the Empress, conceived in the form of a giant Sphinx, thus becoming physically and conceptually immersed in her own creation. Although many dedicated artists and assistants helped the creation and management of the garden it was above all a private and idiosyncratic life journey.

Whatever the motivation of each creator, passion is the compulsive force, over-riding the rational. Many of these gardens were created at great personal expense, physically, mentally, and financially, but these concerns pale into insignificance with the conviction of the artist. For these artists, frequently untrained in any academic sense, the medium of mosaic not only falls easily at the command of such a vision – it encourages it.

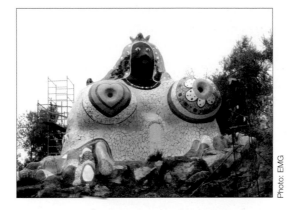

The Empress by Niki de Saint Phalle, Tarot Garden, Tuscany, Italy

A shard of glass is enough to inspire the first steps of such a venture.

Many artists are inspired to create in their own personal space, their home and environment. Works of great poignancy, invention, and energy can result. Each is a unique testament to its creator, often working from an inner compulsion and conviction in a manner outside the conceived norms of aesthetic or generally appreciated understandings. These visions can be raw/ dreamy, and private / exhibitionist – it matters not. It is the driving passion which is the appeal.

# Inspirations from Contemporary Artists

The artists chosen to illustrate mosaic work externally all have one thing in common – they are all visionary. All have turned their unchained visions into reality, working with great passion and long and continuous tenacity. Each has an instinctive and innate aesthetic sensitivity and a great empathy with the external world and environment.

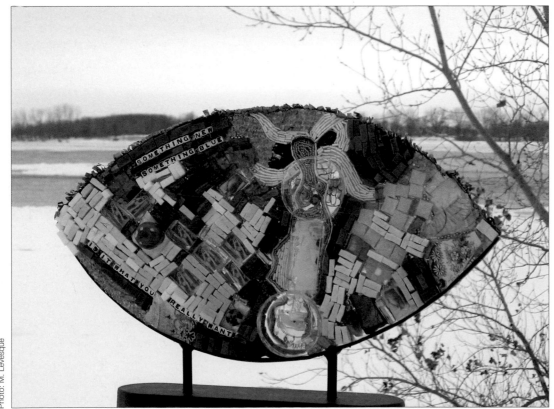

**Mireille Lévesque**
Born in Montreal, Canada, 1949.
Lives and works in Varennes, Canada.

*Artist's Statement, Quebec, Canada, 2007*
I live and work near the St Laurent River in Quebec, Canada. The river and its environment inspires me greatly – birds, waves, seasons. All these elements create a certain rhythm and repetition like musical patterns. In my work I have developed more of a social theme and my approach is humorous and sometimes a bit naïve. The never-ending fight between Nature and Geometry now dominates my work – any happy instants come from the harmony resulting from used materials.

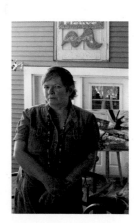

***Something Blue***, 2007
18 x 16in / 46 x 40cm
smalti, china, acrylic,
amethyst, copper

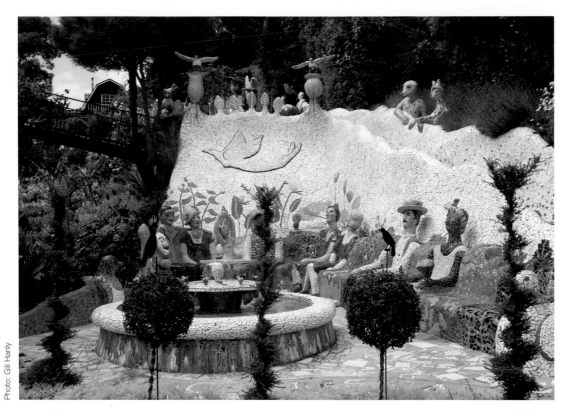

Photo: Gill Hanly

**Josie Martin**
Born in Wellington, New Zealand, 1947.
Lives and works in Akaroa, Banks Peninsula,
New Zealand.

*Artist's Statement, Akaroa, New Zealand, 2007*
Art and Horticulture are dual passions in my life –
one influencing the other. Travel, contemporary
dance, theatre, music – all the arts – stimulate my
creative output. My work is a celebration of life,
firmly optimistic, colorful, eccentric and influenced
by the world around me. I strive to give hope,
inspiration, with the
element of surprise.

***Place des Amis***, 2000,
detail, The Giant's
House, Akaroa,
New Zealand.
tiles, china, glass,
mirror

**Anna Minardo**
Born in Rome, Italy in 1945. Lives and works in
Melbourne, Australia, and in Rome, Italy.

*Artist's Statement, Melbourne, Australia, 2007*
Art is my life. My art is always evolving in a con-
stant search for true essence. I feel the need to
capture the soul of that which I decide to express,
whether through drawing, painting, sculpture or
mosaic. In my mosaic I strive to experience spon-
taneity, integrating the past and the present but
inspired by the ancient flow (*andamento*).

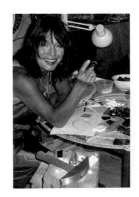

***Mosaic Stream***, 'Oasis',
2005, Waterfront pier,
foreshore, Frankston,
Victoria, Australia,
110m$^2$ (c.130yd$^2$);
South African granite,
marble, colored grout.

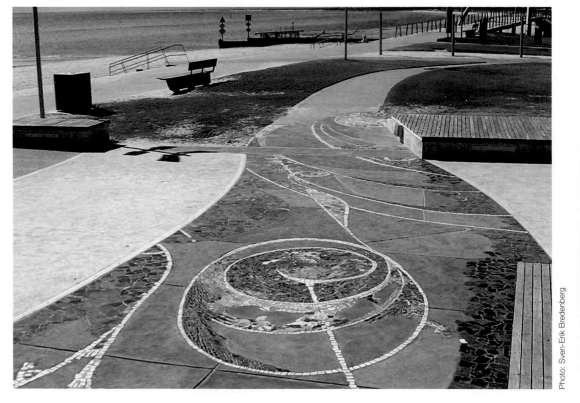

Photo: Sven-Erik Bredenberg

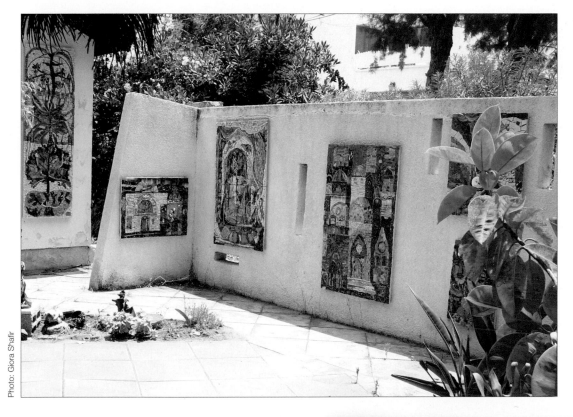

Photo: Giora Shafir

### Ilana Shafir

Born in Sarajevo (former Yugoslavia – now Bosnia and Herzegovina). 1924. Lives and works in Ashkelon, Israel.

*Artist's Statement, Ashkelon, Israel, 2007*
I marvel at the abundance of beauty in our world. I imagine how all of these unique life forms were created and how the world looked when it was first created – primal landscapes, primordial plants and animals in a cosmic womb, waiting to be born into an ever-evolving universe.

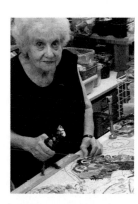

***Primordial Waters;***
***Bird House.***
Detail, garden studio, 2007. Handmade ceramics, painted tiles, cut and natural stones, corals, shells, gold and silver smalti

### Isaiah Zagar

Born Brooklyn, New York, USA, in 1939. Lives and works in Philadelphia USA.

*Artist's Statement, Philadelphia, USA, 2007*
Total embellishment (Demagogic). I desire to change the world into poetic expression. An obsession of sight but not precluding touch and hearing. A follower of the god of adhesion (glue). I'm 68, every day I glue shards on walls on floors on ceilings, inside buildings, outside buildings. A breathless meditation. The rhyme and reason of it within the viewers contemplation.

Hodge podge or Design? Your choice!

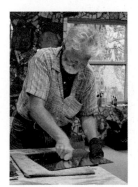

***Sartain St East***, detail, 2007, Philadelphia, USA 4ft x 5ft / 122cm x 152cm; handmade tiles, painted kiln-fired tiles by the artist, mirror, grouted with hand-colored cement

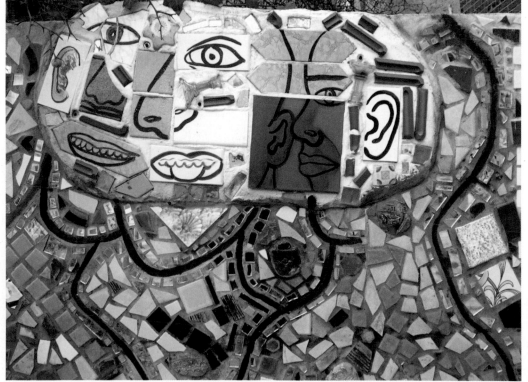

Photo credits: Nikki Miller

# Interior Water Feature

## The Inspirational Mosaic

At the foot of one of the most exquisite buildings I have ever seen – The Secession Building, designed by Josef Maria Olbrich (1867-1908) in Vienna – are two exterior granite pots, with stunning mosaic spiral decoration. Simply conceived, in colors of gold, dark indigo and white, the spirals cascade down the sides, forming complementary introductory features to the jewel of the temple-like building behind them.

*Right: One of two plant holders, by Hans Richard Wustl, 1912, outside the Secession Building, Vienna, Austria*

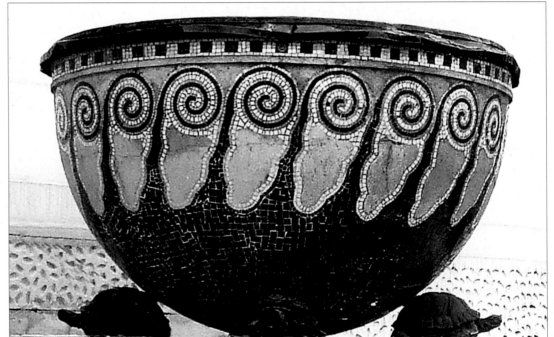

Photo: EMG

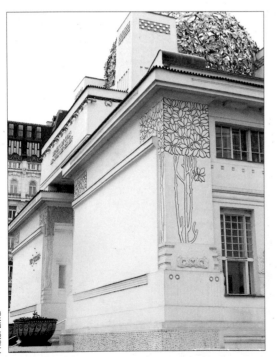

Photo: EMG

## Background Revelations

*Fin de siècle* Vienna was alive with debate and discussion, within the arts of music, literature and the visual arts. In 1897 the artist Gustav Klimt founded the Austrian Secession movement to herald a renewal and reappraisal in Austrian art. This looked towards Art Nouveau and Symbolism for inspiration, converting their free-flowing lines into a more geometric and formal patterning.

*Left: The Secession Building by Josef M Olbrich, 1898-99, Vienna, Austria*

The Secession Building was the movement's headquarters. It was designed by Olbrich with contributions by Klimt. It was a wonderfully liberating building, which rejected established design.

Simple geometric shapes are combined in an unconventional way, using gold and stucco for inspired ornamentation. The two free-standing, very large, mosaic-decorated plant holders, which are positioned on each side of the façade, are exceptional. The use of the spiral in tight and free-flowing forms echoes both the well-ordered classicism and the organic decoration of the building.

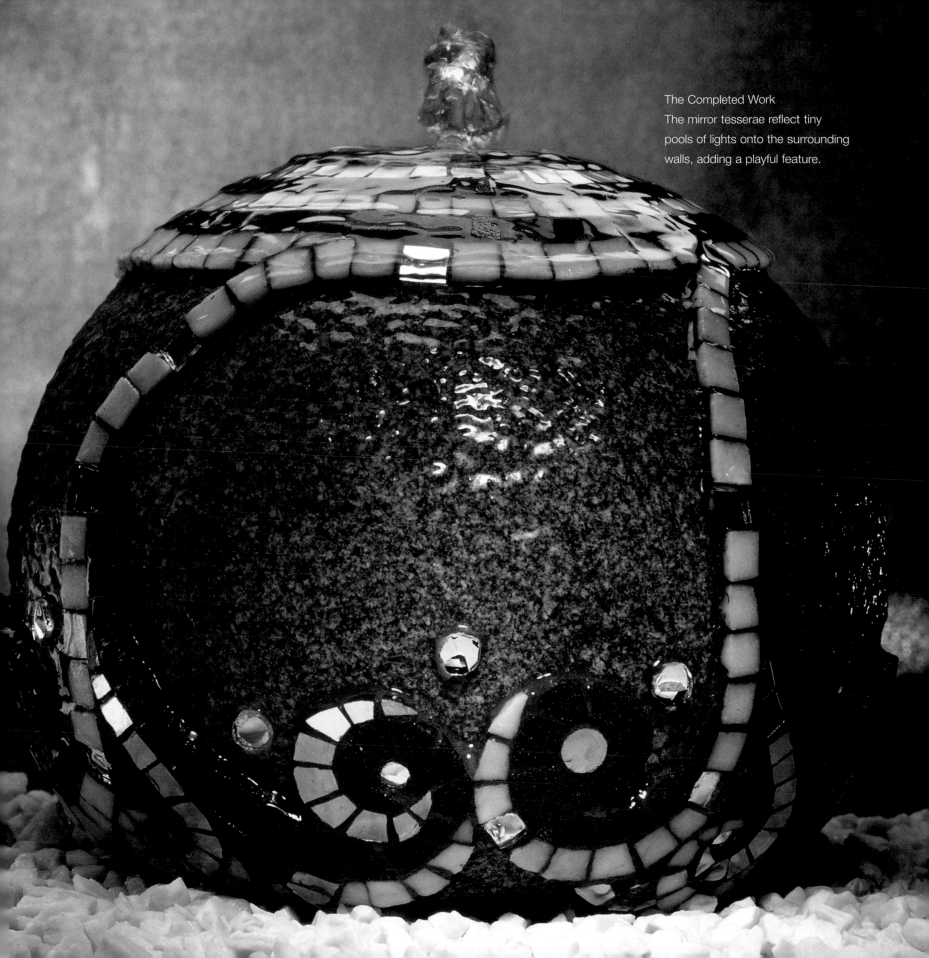

The Completed Work
The mirror tesserae reflect tiny
pools of lights onto the surrounding
walls, adding a playful feature.

# Method

## The Drawing

1 The design begins at the top of the fountain and uses bands of concentric circles to symbolize order and restraint. At four equidistant points, these bands of color give way to random cascades of spirals in gold, deep blue and white, both to symbolize water and to enhance a sense of organic movement and disorder.

## Equipment

| | |
|---|---|
| drawing paper | pencils |
| colored pens | colored pencils |
| tracing paper | |

## Materials

a granite ball 10-12in/25-30cm with a central hole

quick drying waterproof 2-tube resin adhesive

glazed tile for mixing (approx 10 minutes)

plastic spatula

palette

knife

wheeled mosaic nippers

tweezers

prodder

fiber netting

clear plastic sheeting

scissors

old pillow – on which to rest the heavy granite
  ball as it is worked upon

a palette of white and dark blue vitreous glass

Venetian gold leaf glass

mirror tiles

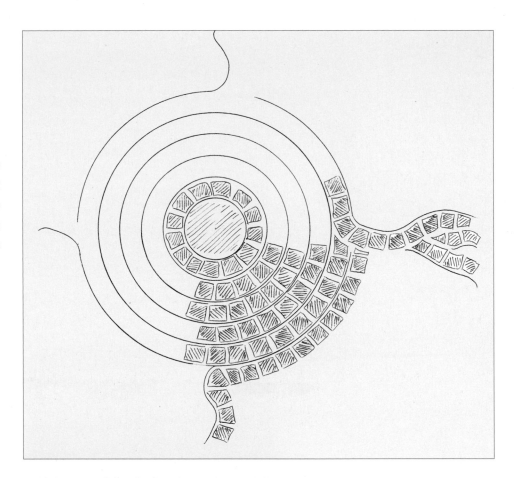

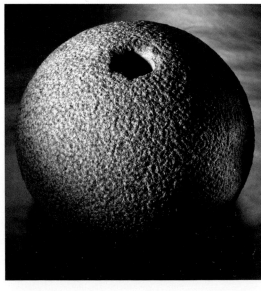

Photo: J. Melvilley

Granite is a beautiful stone, formed of shiny mica, feldspar and quartz.

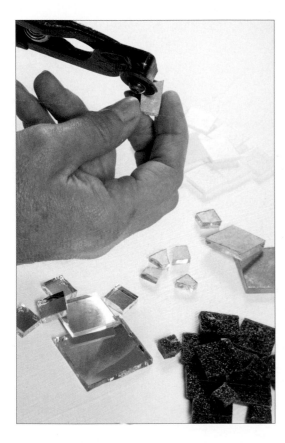

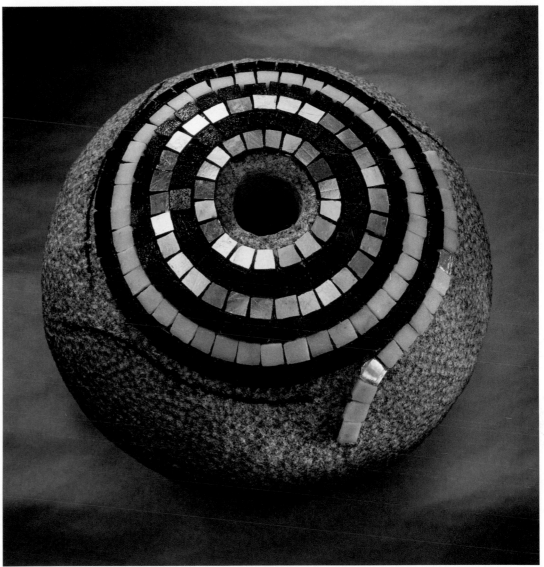

2 The material is cut into four tesserae of fairly regular square shape with occasional tapering to help form the tighter circles of the design.

Taper the tesserae, by cutting one whole tessera in half and angling the nippers to form three tapered shapes from one such half.

3 On a tile, thoroughly mix frequent small and equal quantities of the two-component resin. Use the spatula to apply a little of the mix to the back of each tessera and place on the granite ball. This process can get quite sticky!

Build up the concentric circles around the central hole. At about the seventh concentric circle, in this case a white one, the design begins to fall away into four cascading spirals. At this point begin to add squares of mirror glass.

Photo: J. Melville

4 Divide the ball into four equal sections with a pencil mark and resting the ball on a cushion, draw a design of ornamental spirals in one section. Repeat on all four sides. Trace the design from the ball and work up the drawing with a black marker pen. Transfer the drawing to a sheet of paper and decide on the distribution of the colours.

5 The spiral forms will be repeated four times. Each will be first made on fiber netting before adhering to the granite ball.

Lay the plastic sheeting over the drawing of the spiral, and on top of this the fiber netting. This allows the drawing to be clearly seen while working. The tesserae are cut and adhered to the netting. When completed and secure, turn the mosaic over and leave for a day before peeling off the plastic sheeting. Allow time to dry thoroughly.

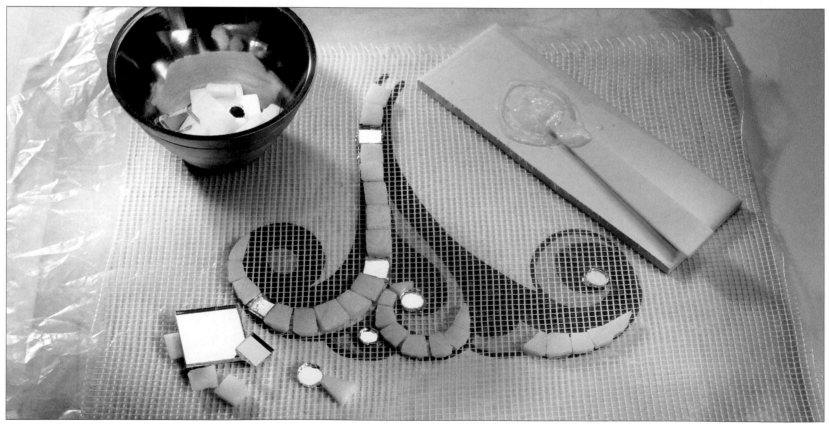

6 Cut the mosaic away from the netting on the reverse side for a closer cut. Use the scissors to cut each mosaic spiral cleanly away from the rest of the netting, and adhere each to the granite ball. Mix a large quantity of the resin and apply to the back of each spiral. Place on the ball, aligning each carefully to the upper part of the mosaic. Hold in position until the resin has 'taken'. This will form a tight waterproof bond.

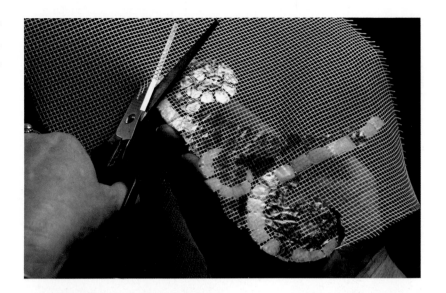

## Grouting and fixing

## Materials

| | |
|---|---|
| ready-mixed exterior cement grout | brushes |
| water | Interior electric water pump |
| containers | approximately 12in/30cm of plastic |
| small trowel | tubing |
| cloths | strong metal grid |
| bowls | white marble chippings (optional) |
| masonry cleaner | wire metal cutters |

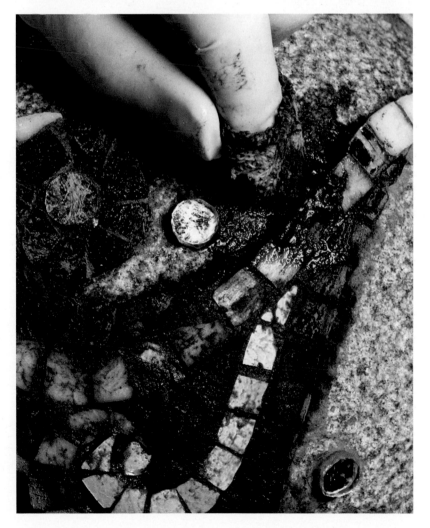

7 When grouting the mosaic, wear protective gloves throughout. Mix up a quantity of the ready-mixed grout – about 2 cups – by cautiously adding water until a fairly stiff mortar is formed. Apply this to the surface of each of the four spiral shapes. The grouting will only cover the mosaic area, as the design does not completely cover the ball – allowing the mosaic medium to complement the granite's strength and beauty – as in the original. Clean carefully using the cloths, and leave under damp cloths to cure.

When the curing process has occurred after two to three days, clean any cement residue by brushing the mosaic surfaces with the masonry cleaner. Be fully protected... Wash clean immediately using large amounts of water. The gleaming surface of the mosaic glass will be exposed.

Fix the electrical pump of the fountain in position as per the manufacturer's instructions, and place the little fountain in position. The pump is concealed by the metal grid which is cut to size and covered with white marble chippings (this allows the mechanism to be hidden from view). Turn on.

# Mirrored Wall Mosaic

## The Inspirational Mosaic

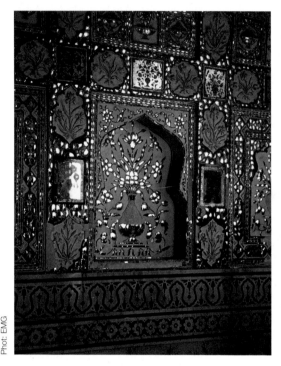

*Mirrored wall mosaic detail, open air ante-chamber, Jai Mandir Palace by Mirza Raja Jai Singh, 1621-1667, Jaipur, Rajasthan, India*

## Background Revelations

Imagine a myriad of sunlit reflections or a veritable kaleidoscope of reflected movement – both my visits in 1983 and 2000 to the Amber fort and palace, just outside in the pink city of Jaipur, offered me such breathtaking visions. The delicately structured ceilings and elegantly refined upper parts of the rooms and open-air chambers

of the Jai Mandir Palace are exquisitely composed of slightly curved gold and silver mirror mosaics. It is entrancing – light dances in a million aspects. This type of mirror work, inspired by the earlier Mughal work of Agra and New Delhi, was employed in India up to the 19th century, and can be seen in many Royal palaces of Rajasthan.

The floral inspiration for the drawing came from two further sources.

The richly colored flowers in the mosaics in the Basilica of San Vitale, with red, orange and white centers, are vibrant in their golden ground. Like the mirror work of India, where light is

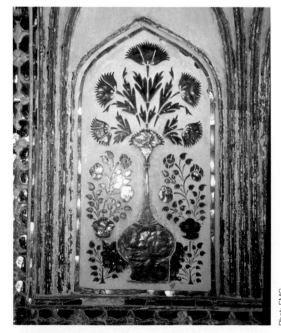

*Flowers and vase, detail, Jai Mandir Palace, 17th century AD. Amber, Jaipur, India*

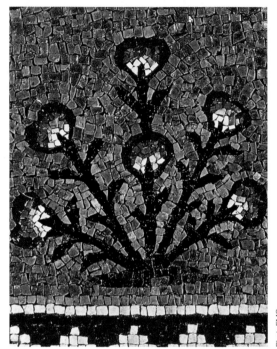

*Flowers, detail, 6th century AD, San Vitale, Ravenna, Italy*

dispersed through curved material for greatest light effect, the Byzantine artists angled the golden glass background tessera in the mortar for greatest play of light on the surface.

In the image of the flowers at Amber, strong colored glass is again used to depict the flower heads – golden glowing blooms. In the background of silvered mirror, each tessera is made up of gently curved glass. When pressed into the mortar, each facet accepts light, viewed from above, in front, and below, giving the maximum possibility for light reflection.

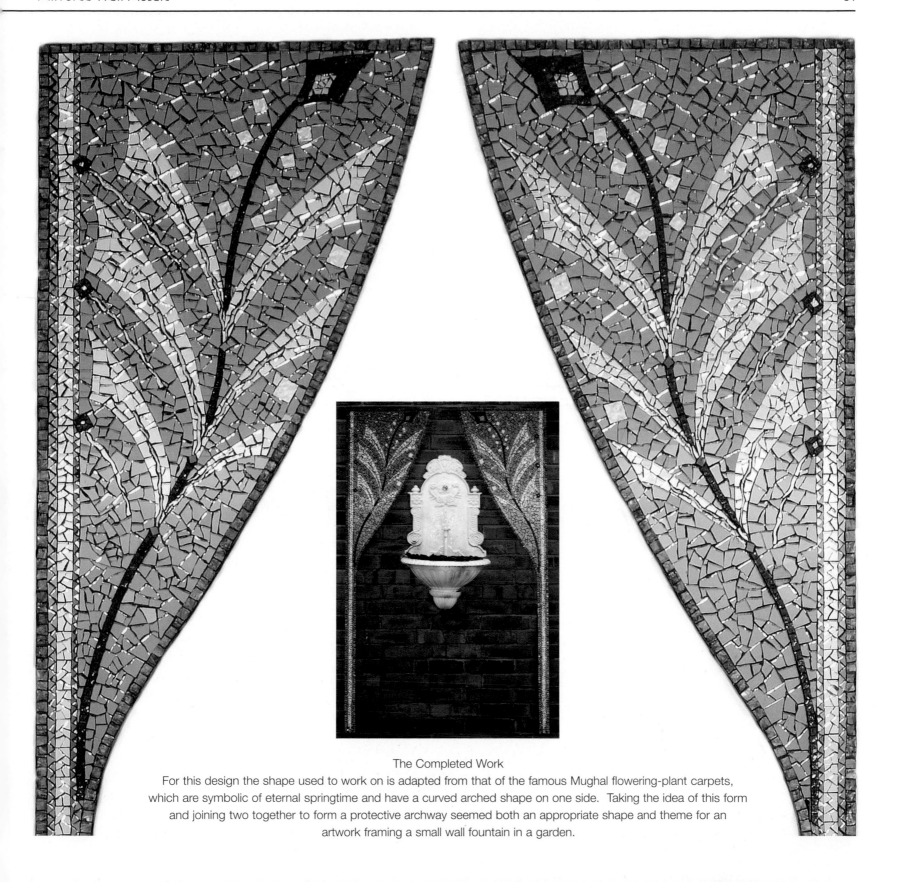

The Completed Work

For this design the shape used to work on is adapted from that of the famous Mughal flowering-plant carpets, which are symbolic of eternal springtime and have a curved arched shape on one side. Taking the idea of this form and joining two together to form a protective archway seemed both an appropriate shape and theme for an artwork framing a small wall fountain in a garden.

## Method

### Preparing the Site

### Equipment

electric drill and masonry bit

plastic screw anchors (Tapits or Rawlplugs)

masonry screws

screwdriver

pencil

First drill the cut timber in position to determine the shape as a whole before attempting the drawing.

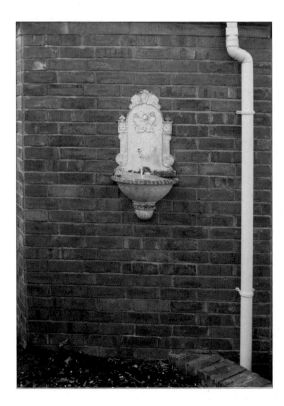

The site – a simple brick wall with a neglected wall fountain.

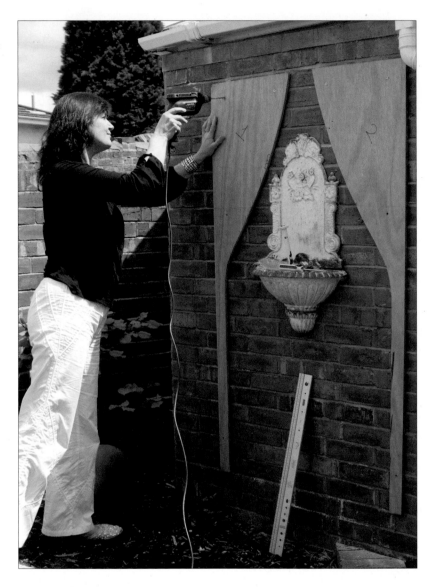

## Materials

½in /12mm marine quality plywood cut to shape, 64in x 16in / 164cm x 40cm

Sheets of standard silver and bronze colored Ravenna mirror glass

copper-colored vitreous glass mosaic (with added copper dust)

plates of Venetian rippled white gold granulated copper-colored Venetian golds

wheeled mirror cutters

pva adhesive / white glue

container

palette knife

ready-mixed cement powder

black cement pigment

small trowel

## The Drawing

## Equipment

pencils

carbon paper

felt-tipped marker pen

brushes

eraser

gold and silver inks

tracing paper

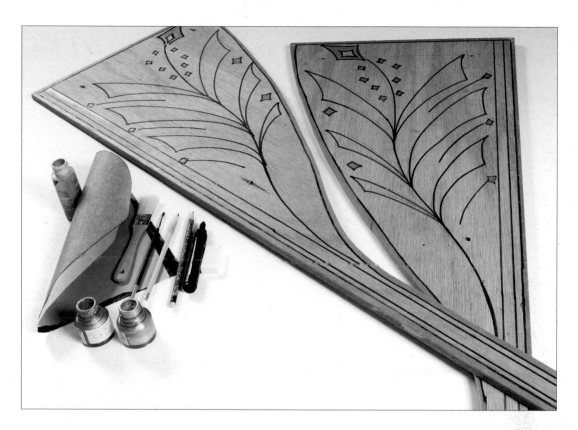

1 The drawing was made directly onto the timber backing for the mosaic. One side, the left-hand side, of the arch was drawn in pencil and firmed up with a marker pen. Part of this drawing, the flower section, was then traced over using large sheets of tracing paper.

When completed, these were turned upside-down and placed in position on the right-hand board in a corresponding position. Sheets of carbon paper were placed between the traced drawing and the timber, and the flower section re-drawn in reverse. The drawing on timber was again firmed up with the marker pen. The border edges were defined, using a straight-edge ruler, directly onto the timber.

Use inks to mark the areas for color reference. This is a guide only, and it helps when considering the palette color and materials to be chosen.

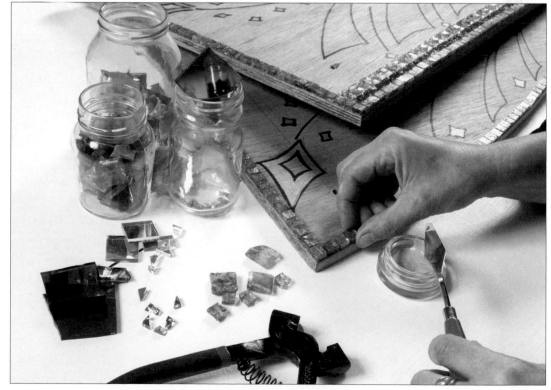

2 Cut the iridescent copper vitreous tiles into four and using the adhesive, fix them to the outer edge of the two panels. Create a decorative geometric design on the outer edges which will fill completely the lower part of the timber, i.e. the side lengths.

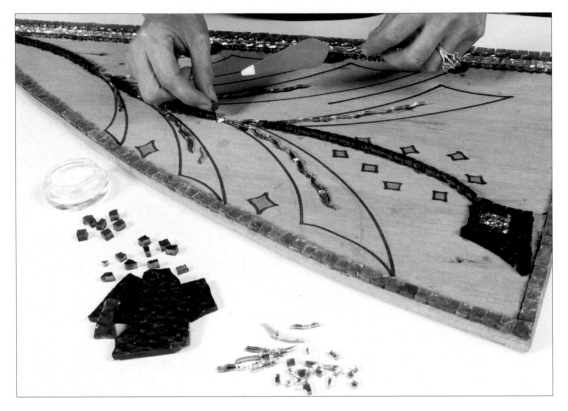

3 Apply small tesserae cubes, using the Venetian golds to form the two stems of the flowers. At intervals, use a different color of copper gold. Begin to fix the leaf spines using mirror glass in small tesserae shapes and longer curved shapes. These are adhered directly onto the plywood backing timber.

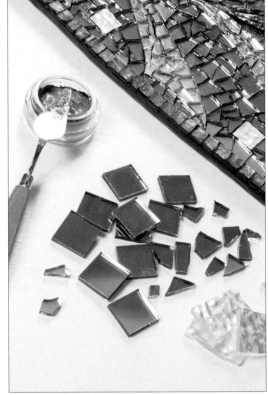

4 Fill in the leaf-forms with mirror mosaic. The mirror is not curved as in the original in India, but to create the effect of a more dramatic light refraction, add some cement powder to the pva/white glue adhesive in a container, and add a quarter-teaspoonful of cement pigment. Mix this well. Trowel the pigmented adhesive onto the board in small quantities, after first applying a thin layer of adhesive by brush to form both a sealer and a strong contact layer. The mirror tesserae are then pressed into this at gently varying angles.

Cut squares of Venetian white gold (silver) and create areas of decorative interest near the top of the central flower, and also towards the outer frame. These will help lift the background, adding points of dense bright light.

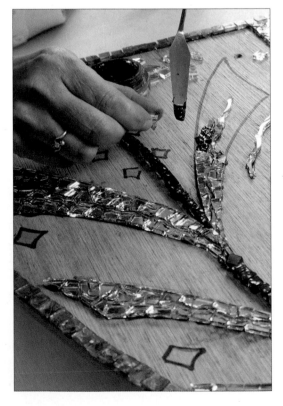

5 The mosaic is then completed using the bronzed mirror, in the crazy-paving way of laying the tesserae known as *opus palladianum*. The tesserae can be fairly large and carefully aligned in the pigmented textured adhesive to form a multi-faceted ground to catch light from all directions.

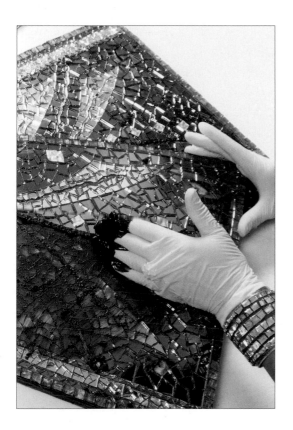

## Materials

proprietary ready-mixed fine grout

black cement pigment

trowel

cloths

containers

water

silicon polishing cloth (one used for window
   or glass cleaning)

protective gloves

black waterproof wood sealer

palette knife

brush

long screws and screwdriver

hanging tesserae

## Grouting and Hanging

6 Wearing gloves, put a quantity of the cement mix in a container and add about a level tea-spoon of cement pigment – this is a very dense, light permanent pigment, made specifically for coloring cement. Mix well together, then add water slowly until a uniform and pliable mortar is formed. Rub this into the whole surface of the mosaic, carefully rubbing over the very slightly angled surfaces. When certain that all the gaps are grouted, use the cloth to rub off the excess mix. Be sure to clean the areas around the hang-ing holes carefully, then leave the two mosaics to cure under damp cloths for three days. When the curing process is completed, use a polishing cloth to buff up the mirror to a natural gleam.

Seal the edges of the mosaics using a black proprietary waterproof sealer to completely cover the cut edge. A palette knife is a very useful tool with which to apply the sealer and to smooth it in position.

Use the brush to apply a waterproof wood sealer to cover the back of the work, to secure it from any possible humid conditions when placed externally.

Carry the newly-created mosaics to the site, which has been somewhat tidied and the metal fountain de-rusted and repainted.

Place the works against the wall and hang them securely into their pre-drilled positions, using the screwdriver. The drilled holes can be countersunk if preferred, to enable the final filling tesserae to lie flat to the surface for complete camouflaging. Leaving the hanging tesserae to lie proud of the surface, however, will enable quick and easy identification, should the work need to be taken down or transferred.

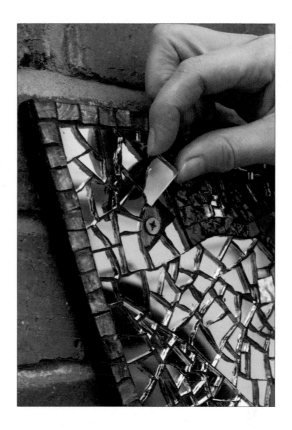

7 Cut single tesserae to fit the shape of the areas left after hanging the work, and adhere them in position, completing the mosaic *in situ*. These small areas can be grouted (if required) using a little of the same grout mortar as prepared for the main grout.

Polish the mosaic with a final buffing using a silicon cloth – the mirror will sparkle in the outdoor light to great effect.

# Lounger

## The Inspirational Mosaic

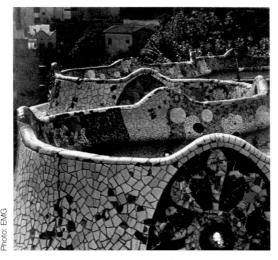

The Serpentine Bench (detail)[1], designed by Antoni Gaudì (1852-1926), decorative application by Josep M Jujol (1879-1949), Parc Güell, Barcelona, Spain, 1910-1913

## Background Revelations

When I first visited the glorious coastal city of Barcelona, and the Parc Güell in the late 1970s, I remember gasping with delight on seeing the undulating mosaic bench of color and light unfolding before me. It was a revelation – mosaic could be sculptural, external and made of discarded materials! Liberating!

[1]The photo shows the bench before restoration (photo 1990)

The great Catalan architect/designer Antoni Gaudì came from a family of goldsmiths. From a young age he venerated both the skill of the artisan and the power of Nature – from which he gleaned inspiration for both structural and decorative detailing. A further inspiration for Gaudì in surface decoration came from Spain's Islamic past, which resulted in him creating with great effect applied decoration of multi-colored tiling, often coupling it with neo-mediaeval structures.

There is an underlying rationale in all Gaudì's work, into which he puts passion through both poetic and sometimes dark energy. The temple church of Sagrada Familia is a living witness to his creative force. A fortunate collaboration was with Josep Maria Jujol, a young draftsman and architect whom Gaudì allowed free expression in the decoration of the serpentine bench which tops the so-called "Hall of 100 Columns" (there are in fact 86). The bench was made up of prefabricated parts. The profile and measurements, it is said, derived from those taken from a cast of a seated naked workman.

Jujol's work is masterly. The base of his work is composed of white and light-colored tiles and china, whose glazed multi-facetted surfaces radiate light in both the sunshine and the rain. Parabolic arches of motifs of decorative colored tiles are interspersed along the serpentine bench. Materials of glass, hand-painted china discs, ceramic, bottle glass and the occasional doll parts create a living surface of texture and interest.

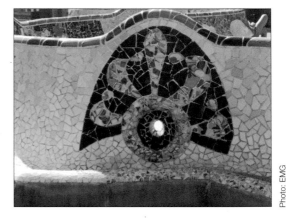

The Serpentine Bench after restoration (detail) showing drainage holes and the replaced colored top coving

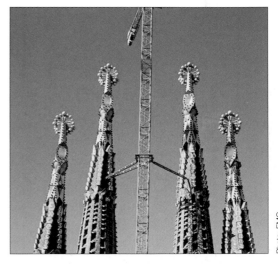

The four spires of the temple of Sagrada Familia by A. Gaudi, Barcelona, Spain, are silhouetted against the sky. The central building crane denotes the fact that the building is unfinished and is in a continuing state of creation, begun in 1911 and on-going

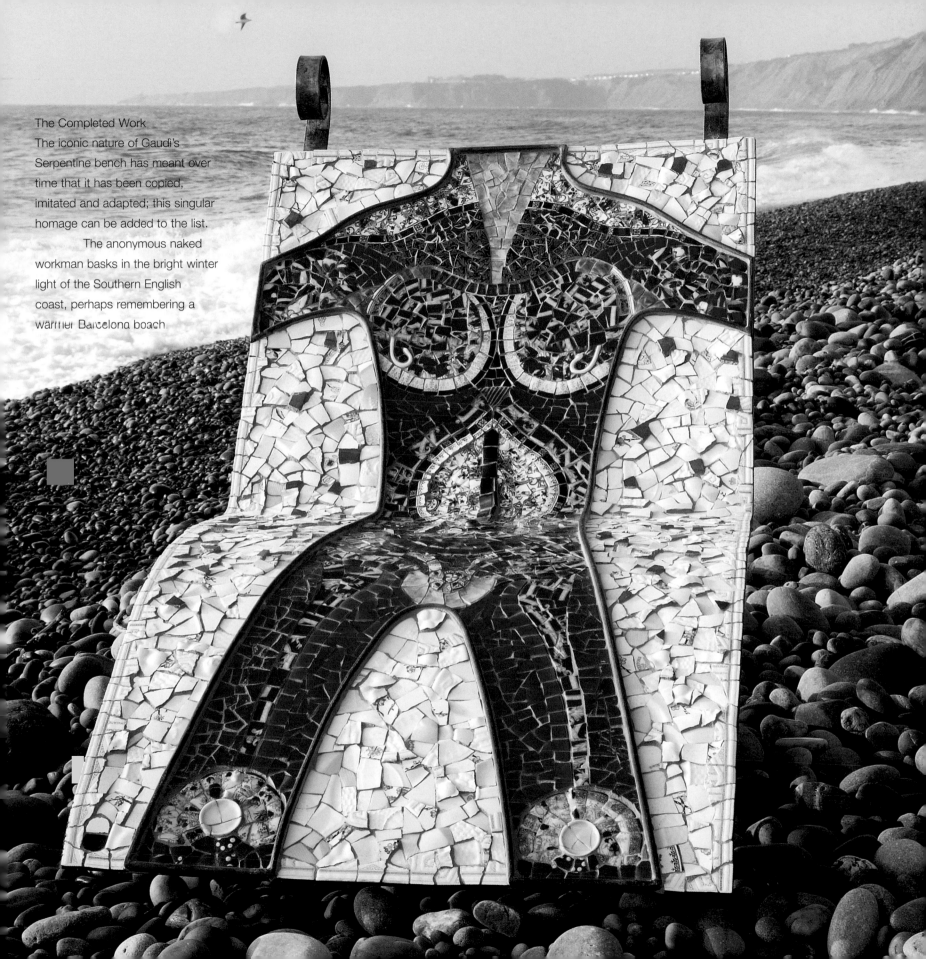

The Completed Work
The iconic nature of Gaudi's
Serpentine bench has meant over
time that it has been copied,
imitated and adapted; this singular
homage can be added to the list.
    The anonymous naked
workman basks in the bright winter
light of the Southern English
coast, perhaps remembering a
warmer Barcelona beach

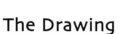

# Method

## About the Design

The concept for this design was inspired by the knowledge that Antonì Gaudì had used the posture of a naked workman cast in plaster to give rise to the profile that forms the shape of the Serpentine Bench in Parc Güell. I wished to acknowledge this anonymous workman.

The Lounger base is made from galvanized metal with a drawn male metal figure, outlined in applied metal to my own design. The original metal work is by Les Clifton and the galvanizing and additional metal figure work are by Richard Bent.

## The Drawing

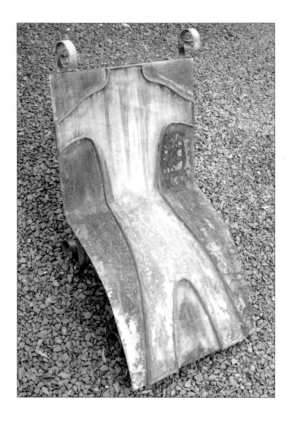

## Materials and Equipment

All the materials used in this work will be what is known in Spain as *trencadis* – discarded china, tiles and pottery
pencils
brush container
proprietary fast flex cement
slant-edged palette knife
standard mosaic nippers and wheeled mosaic nippers
water

*Below*: A selection of materials – china, tiles, porcelain, and miscellaneous items – collected for the design in shades of terracotta, burnt sienna, and orange / pinks, and white.

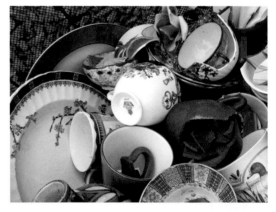

There will be a spontaneous, joyous feel to this work, dictated in part by the imagery, the naked workman – and partly by the capricious nature of the materials. However, a pencil or two at hand that will show up well on the galvanized metal will be a useful adjunct, when working out the limitations of the area to be worked on.

The cement used throughout to affix the material to the metal chair will be a fast flex cement, i.e., one that is suitable for adhering

ceramic to metal. It is fairly easily obtainable and is a two component adhesive: (1) a rubber-based crumb powder, and (2) a polymer liquid. These are mixed together according to the instructions, and can be obtained in white or gray. Although white is not the best color to enhance materials when used as a grout color, the fixing cement will be covered up – I have used white to show up the tesserae more clearly against the gray galvanized steel of the chair.

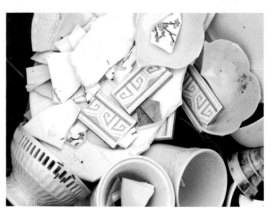

### Secret Insight 1
The Parc Güell Serpentine Bench is a magnificent work but sadly, in terms of seating, it does not lend itself to more than a few moments of relaxation. An uncomfortable ceramic protuberance runs along the central curve of the upper back and discourages a longer stay.

1 Putting a little of the cement on the back of each tessera before securing it in position. Use the palette knife to apply the mix to each tessera before fixing in position. Enjoy the process. Marvel at the textures, colors and glazes of your chosen miscellaneous materials – this joy is apparent in all Jujol's *trencadis* work.

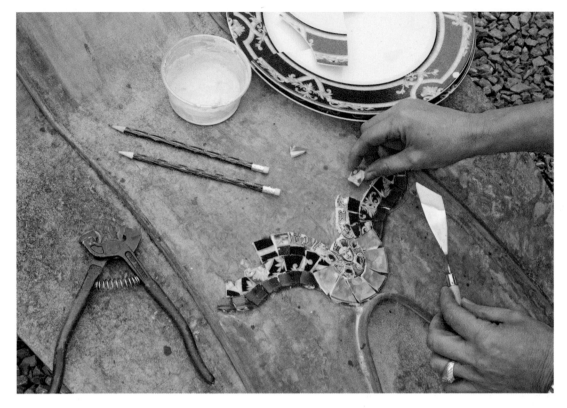

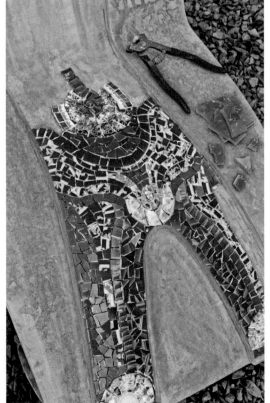

2 Apply a rich medley of colors and materials to the lower part of the male form. It was easier to work on the lower part of the torso first, as this is the seat of the lounger. It is unlikely that many will be courageous enough to sit on the seat so I have allowed free rein to the heights of the material used – the stage of grouting will even out some of the raised edges.

**Secret Insight 2**

For many years Jujol was unrecognized as the ingenious artist behind the extraordinary mosaic work in Barcelona. All was, until recently, attributed to Gaudì, although a signature appears on the bench, but this was only found when the work was reconditioned for the Olympic Games in Barcelona in 1992.

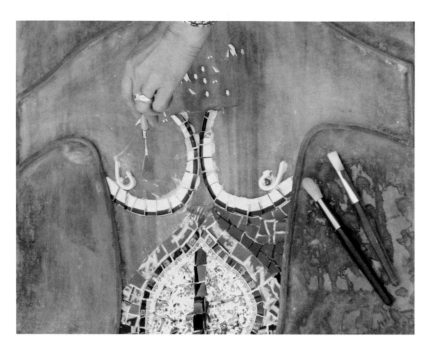

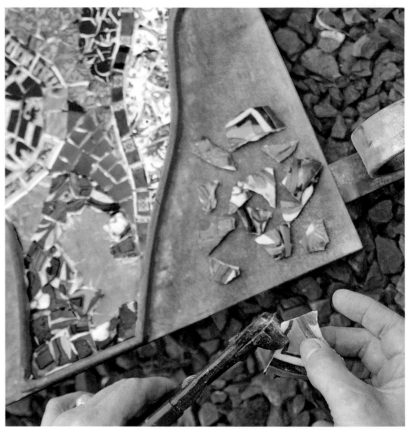

3 Cleaning away excess cement using a slant-edged palette knife. The brushes are used to clear away any shards left by the cutting technique. Sort through the materials, ruthlessly editing out anything which you feel will not enhance your palette of colors. I have chosen colors in the orangey/pink brown/terracotta range, an exaggerated pigment homage to the human skin color of the mythical workman.

4 Working on the shoulder area. Tip the lounger up to rest on its back when working on the chest and neck area. The delight of working in discarded *trencadis* is to take full advantage of their surface designs and markings. Sometimes specific reference can be taken from the decoration on the china – words, pictures, and dates. Also the form of the crockery may come into play in the design – a cup handle, a knob of a teapot lid, an edging rim, a repeated gilt pattern can all be used to contain or define the form in a novel way, to be exploited at leisure.

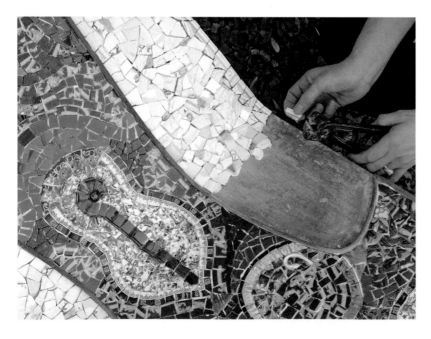

5 The colorful silhouette of the figure will be placed on a white background – also the favored color choice of Jujol. Create an edging border before filling in with a mix of white-colored china and tile. Tiles originally manufactured to make a decorative frieze were cut into tesserae and used to create a good straight edging for the lounger. The background area was then filled in with a motley assortment of textured and high gloss white *trencadis*. Here and there a gold tile was added and a complementary tessera or two of an orange or red color. These "accidentals" enrich an otherwise single-colored area.

## Grouting

## Materials

a proprietary super flex grouting powder,
  or a standard wide-joint grouting powder
  plus a polymer additive
heavy duty protective gloves
bowls
cloths
mixing trowel

water
mortar
cleaner
brush
plastic container
masonry brush or other
medium-firm brush

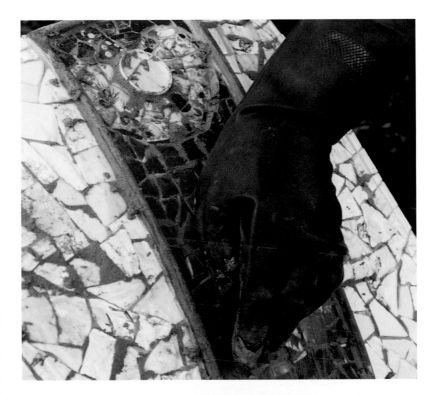

6  The lounger might be sat upon, so it is important to use a grout which will adapt to some flexing of the steel – a super flex wall grout or a standard grouting powder to which a polymer liquid can be added can both work well in these conditions.

Wear the protective gloves, and put a quantity of the cement grout into a large bowl – about six mugfuls. Add the polymer and water, mixed together in a ratio of 1:1, and mix to a fairly moist mortar. The liquid polymer is a cement additive. It creates a more malleable mortar and a grout more resistant to flexing.

Press into all the interstices, taking care over the raised edges of some materials. This procedure may take some time. Grouting such a textured surface is never a rushed job, but the final effects are worth the labor. When the grouting is completed, leave under damp cloths for 3 to 4 days to cure slowly. This process may take a little longer as the gaps are wider – a long slow cure time can only be beneficial.

Clean off any excess cement scum with a brushing down of a proprietary mortar cleaner which contains hydrochloric acid (HCl). The cement will "fizz" on application and come away easily.

Wash with large amounts of water and allow to dry naturally.

Use the masonry brush or other fairly firm-bristled brush to polish the surface, cleaning away excess mortar. Persevering with the brushing will result in a surface gleaming with color and reflected light.

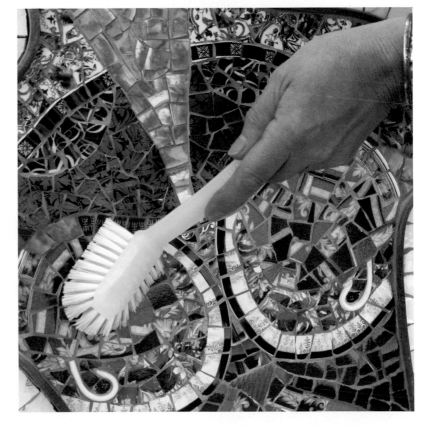

# Courtyard Entranceway

## The Inspirational Mosaic

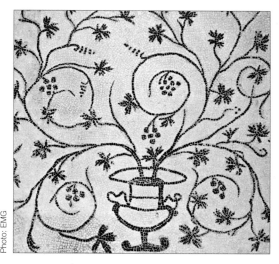

Photo: EMG

*Krater with Vine and Tendrils, 24in x 24in / 60cm x 60cm, 2nd-3rd century AD, Uzitta, Tunisia, now in the Sousse Archaeological Museum, Tunisia*

## Background Revelations

One of the most ubiquitous motifs on many a Roman mosaic is the *krater*, a wine drinking or mixing vessel often depicted with vine branches emanating from it. Some mosaics, using this image for decorative effect, cover vast expanses with intricate polychrome mosaic which play their part superbly in scenes of Dionysiac revel.

The one I have chosen, however, is one of the smallest, simplest monochrome depictions I know of – and I adore it – it is my inspiration.

The naiveté of the design, the slight hesitation of the tesserae movement, and the delight in the essential elements of the motif produce a freely drawn image which gives great pleasure. The enlacing form of vine shoots, with simplified bunches of grapes and coiled tendrils rising from a full cup, intoxicates my senses and makes me muse on who might have made this mosaic – *not* a master mosaic draftsman (a *pictor imaginarius*), *not* a master mosaic worker (a *musivarius*) but a local citizen eager to make a mosaic himself – well versed in the imagery but with access only to black and white tesserae and an enquiring eager mind – dear reader – you?

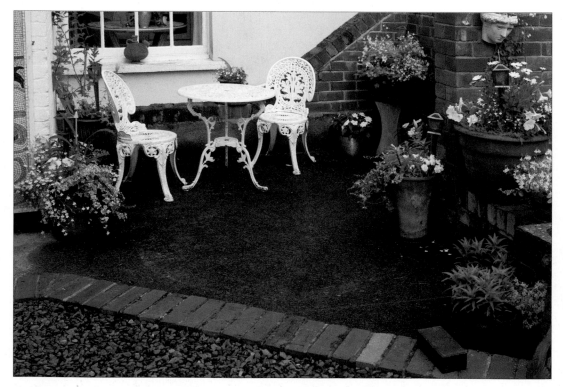

*A much-loved courtyard, decorated with flowering pots to mask the bare-floored setting (an example of a gray paver can be seen bottom right)*

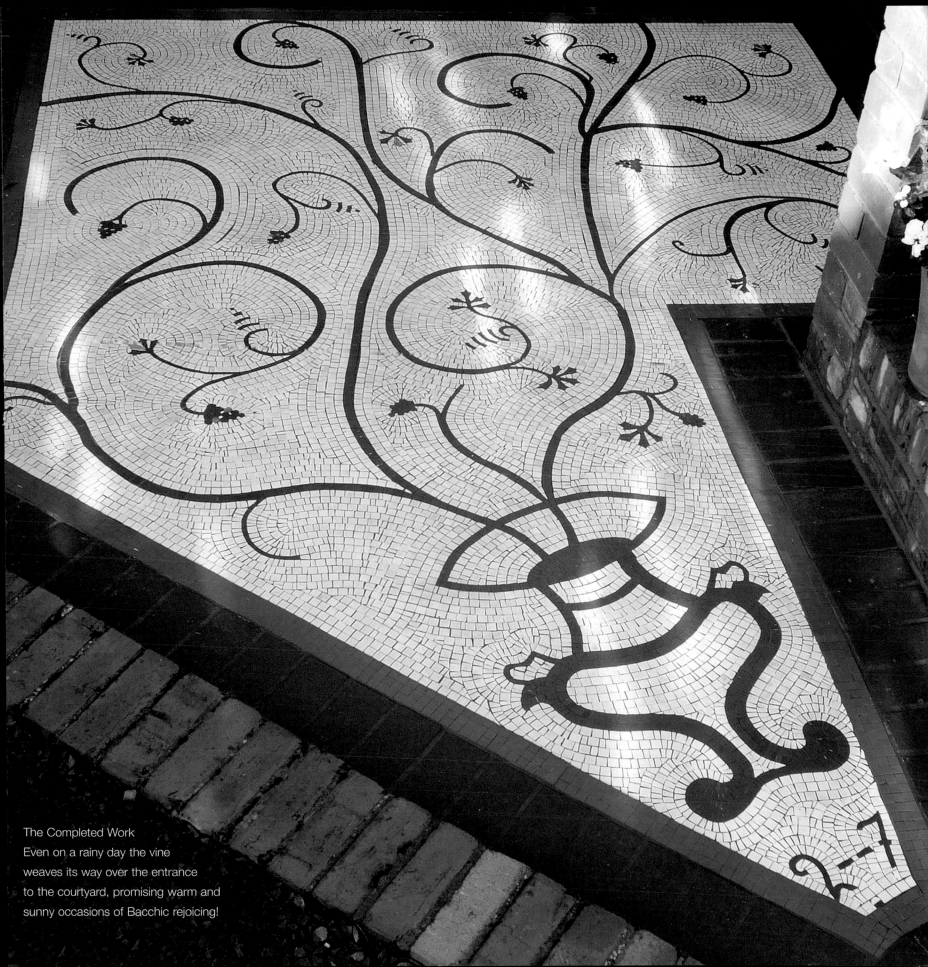

The Completed Work
Even on a rainy day the vine
weaves its way over the entrance
to the courtyard, promising warm and
sunny occasions of Bacchic rejoicing!

## Method

### Preparing the Site

1 The foundation of bare concrete was sound enough in itself to act as a foundation for a mosaic.  Two expert paving constructors were asked to both create a frame for the mosaic in charcoal gray concrete pavers, and to raise the level of the ground on which to construct the mosaic.

Wayne first cuts the pavers into tapering shapes with a disc cutter.  These will be laid vertically as "soldiers" and form a framing border.

Using a rubber hammer, he then taps the pavers firmly into position in a fan-shaped design. The interstices are filled with a golden-colored kiln-dried sand.

Finally, Thomas fills the area remaining with a mortar of sand and cement  in a ratio of 4:1.  Using a metal float he smoothes the surface, leaving a level approximately ½in/1cm below the height of the surrounding pavers.

A few days later... after the concrete has slowly cured, I am able to sand the area down with an emery cloth.  It's quite a labor!

From time to time, where small lumps of concrete have occurred, these are chiseled off using a hammer and a broad-angled chisel.  The area is brushed clean after the sanding to provide a good finish on which to create a mosaic work.

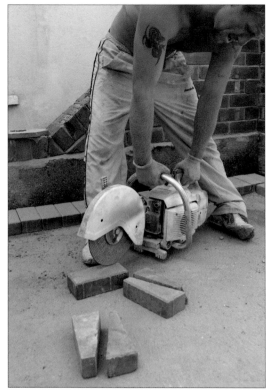

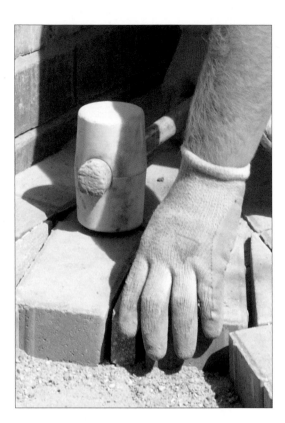

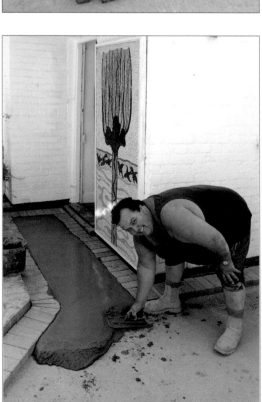

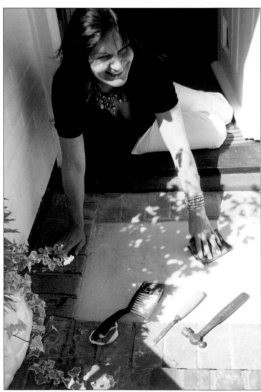

## Drawing Equipment

*Conté* crayons
fixative spray
kneeling pad

2 Drawing the scrolling vines freely to fit the pre-required shape. I wanted to use the simplest of materials to create a fairly spontaneous image, which would adapt to the irregular shape of the area to be worked on, in order to strike an empathy with the designer of the original mosaic. Allow the vine to emanate from the open cup or krater from two stems; this gives two possible directions for the design.

Conté crayon is lovely to draw with, and it adheres fairly well to the concrete. Draw only the simplest of branches; details such as leaves and bunches of grapes can be added later.

Fix the drawing with a proprietary fixative, or even hair spray. In the wet climate this was a necessary precautionary procedure.

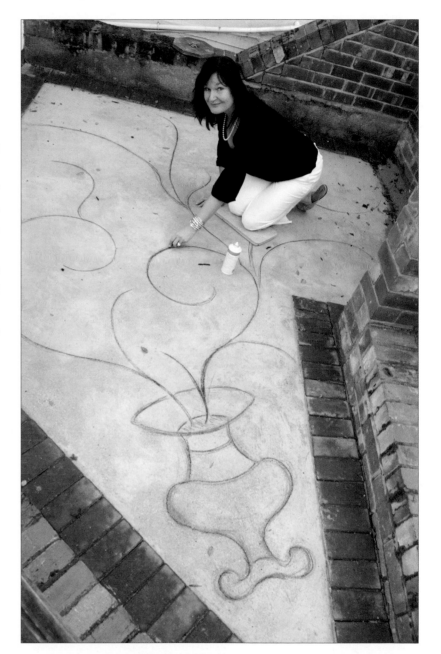

## Materials and Equipment

| | |
|---|---|
| black unglazed ceramic tesserae | ready mix cement adhesive |
| white unglazed ceramic tesserae | trowel |
| green unglazed ceramic floor tesserae | water |
| Venetian gold and green gold leaf glass | gloves |
| proprietary quick-setting grouting powder | cloths |
| pva adhesive/white glue | bowls |
| various containers | flexible palette knife |
| palette knife | round-edged palette knife |
| permanent marker pen | mortar |
| fiber netting | cleaner |
| plastic | container |
| sheeting | brush |
| strong brown wrapping paper | gloves |
| pencils | a large board of plywood |
| scissors | hammer |
| standard mosaic nippers | |

**Secret Insight 1**
Using a frame of dark-colored tesserae introduces the mosaic work by visually easing in the smaller size of tile, which is such a contrasting size to the larger pavers. The Romans often employed this feature, one which both retains and frames the mosaic work and connects it with a room or floor area into which it is laid.

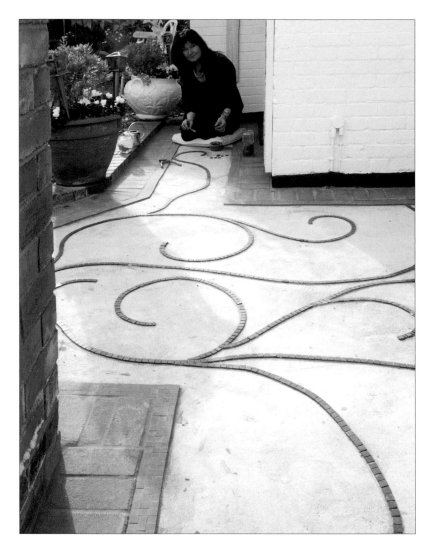

3 Build up the vine using black ceramic tesserae in a simple flowing design. Place a quantity of the ready-mixed cement adhesive in a container, add water and mix to make a moist mortar. Trowel a little of this onto each tessera (or lay a thin layer of mortar onto the ground, smoothing the surface), and place the green tesserae in framing lines. The ground surface should be dry and clean of dust, so brush the surface before applying the mortar. Frame all the area which is to contain the mosaic design. With the onset of inclement weather, I needed to grout and secure the border before beginning on the mosaic. The frame was also cursorily cleaned with mortar cleaner before work continued.

It was hoped that the work could be made totally *in situ* – as is so obviously the original inspirational mosaic. However, England's erratic weather put a stop to this and the mosaic was made both on site and in the studio, as weather conditions permitted.

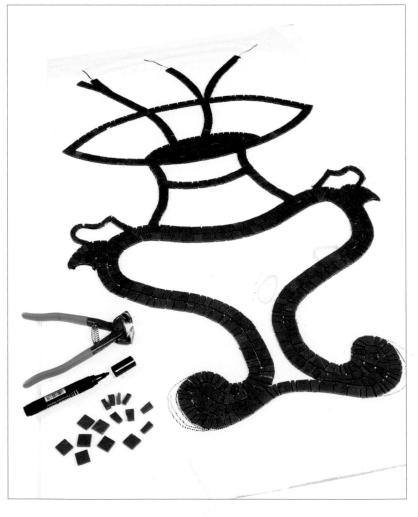

4 The *krater* was made up in the studio, but to transfer the drawing, plastic sheeting was placed over the drawing of the *krater* in the courtyard, and the outline loosely drawn on it. This drawing was then taken inside and put on the worktable and covered with fiber netting. The krater was outlined with whole black tesserae, occasionally cut to shape to help define the image. A little adhesive was placed on the back of each tile before adhering it to the netting – the drawing on the plastic could be clearly seen and easily followed.

The *krater* was in-filled with white ceramic tesserae; many were left whole, while others were cut in half or shaped to help define any curving contours, e.g., around the krater handles. Up to about a meter in size was created; this is about the maximum size to securely allow lifting and carrying to site with such a design.

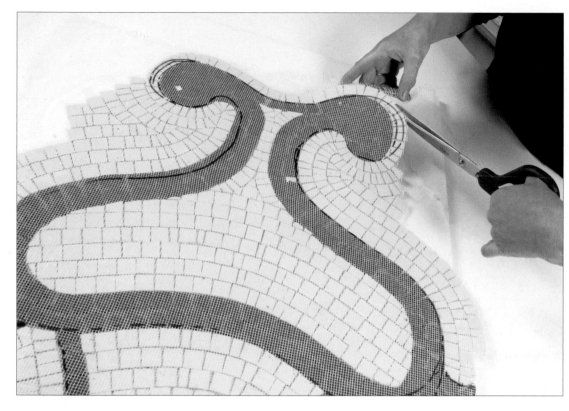

5 When the mosaic was completed and dry, it was cut to shape and the excess fiber netting removed.

The mosaic on its netting was then carried outside and turned over. The back was covered with a thin layer of cement adhesive and troweled smooth. Special care was taken at the edge pieces. The whole was then placed right side up in position on the concrete foundation.

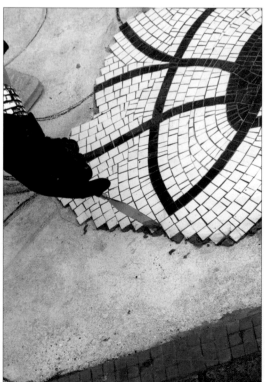

6 Any excess mortar was cleaned away with a round-edged palette knife. A large board of ¼in/6mm plywood was laid over the whole design and gently tapped with a hammer to ensure a flat, even surface.

The mosaic *krater* was slightly out of line with the initial drawing because additional layers of surrounding white tesserae at the base meant the mosaic was placed fractionally higher than originally envisaged. These changes in mosaic creation happen – adapt to them, never force rigid interpretations unless space is at a premium. The design is a loosely flowing one – the growing vine. Enjoy developing it visually as it progresses.

The vine continued to be drawn in uncut black ceramic tesserae to a loosely flowing pattern. Use a little of the proprietary cement adhesive in a container, and add water and mix to a fairly moist consistency. With a flexible palette knife, apply a little of the adhesive to the back of each tile before firmly placing in position. Do not adjust the tiles after placing; the newly-concreted foundation will rapidly absorb the moisture and any movement will weaken the initial grip. Cut away the excess mortar after each application, using the side edge of the palette knife. The *rinceau* or curved design of the vine shoots will form conveniently-sized areas creating natural templates which can be worked on in the studio.

7 The black mosaic outlines of the vine give secure outer edges for each template. Occassionally a black tile may come loose, but the overall outline will remain.

8 Draw up the design on the brown paper templates using a black marker pen, adding simply-drawn vine leaves, tendrils and bunches of grapes wherever this feels appropriate. Keep the drawing spontaneous and simplify all the shapes. Put a sheet of clear plastic over the drawing, and add enough fiber netting to cover the drawing. When each section is completed, allow it to dry before turning over and peeling off the plastic.

Allow each mosaic template to dry thoroughly before transferring them to the site. Each is adhered to the ground using the cement adhesive. Remember to clean up the edges after laying each template, to allow for a tight abutting when laying the next.

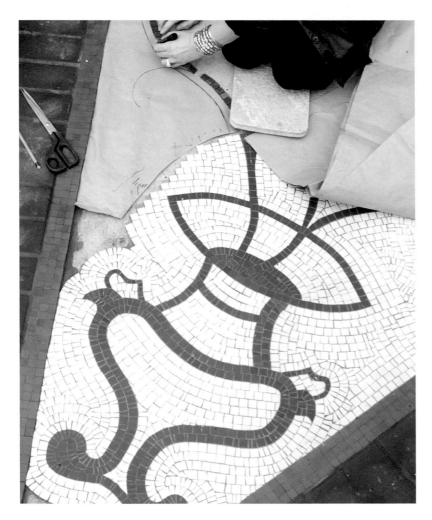

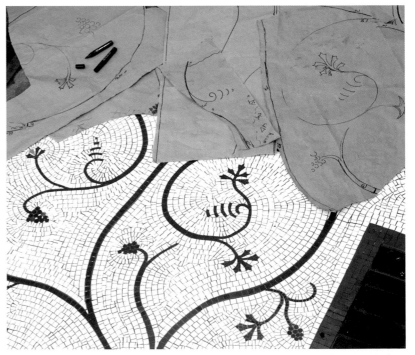

9 Because of the bitterly cold conditions, torrential rain and even nightly freezing temperatures, I needed to grout each section after laying it, using a fast-setting cement adhesive, and then cover it with plastic overnight. Frost is not conducive to cement work – but a deadline for the finish of this book was calling… The mosaic continued to be made both at site and using templates.

From time to time in the making of the mosaic leaves and grapes, a few pale Venetian gold or green Venetian gold leaf tesserae were added. In the oncoming spring and summer sunshine these few tesserae will glint and sparkle. Including gilded tesserae in this manner not only adds interest to the simple design but also alludes to the intriguing use of gold in Roman mosaics.

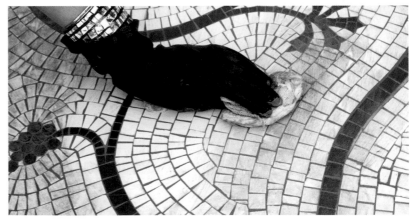

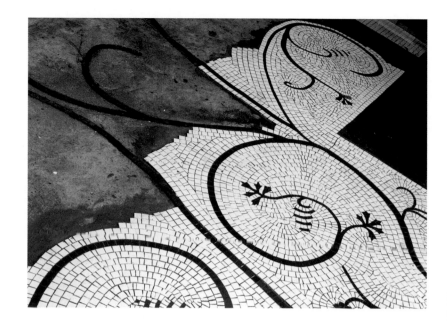

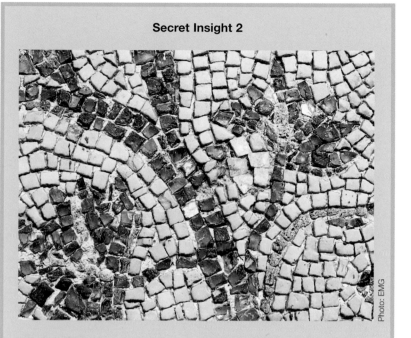

Photo: EMG

**Secret Insight 2**

*Vine mosaic, detail, showing occasional tesserae of translucent backing glass (formerly gilded), 2nd-3rd century AD, Antioch / Antakya Museum, Turkey*

10 Continue to build up the mosaic. The process is a long but enjoyable one – it now becomes understandable why the Romans employed an organic design of this kind so frequently in their floor pavements around the Mediterranean. There is something immensely satisfying about working in this very free form way, while adhering to the simplest tenets of mosaic making – I only envy the Mediterranean climate.

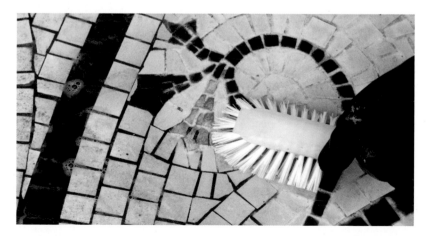

11 On completion allow the mosaic to cure a few days before re-grouting the whole work. This is a unifying procedure, securely grouting the joining areas where each successive template has been added, and also where the initial grouting has been a little rushed or inadequate in the inclement conditions. Clean the excess grout away then carefully clean the whole surface with mortar cleaner. Thoroughly rinse and leave to dry naturally.

Since Roman Imperial times, gilded glass is known to have been used in mosaic work. But this is very, very rarely seen. The most plausible reason could be that the cartellina or thin top layer of glass that covered the gold leaf has weathered away and taken the fragile gold leaf also, leaving only the clear or pale green backing glass. This backing glass appears to look like stone or marble and can easily be overlooked, specially so as the work was often on a dark cement foundation.

On a recent visit to view (scrutinize) the mosaics of Antioch/Antakya in Hatay Museum in Turkey, where some of the floor mosaics are also displayed as wall panels, light from the great museum's windows revealed the glint of clear glass tesserae in such a mosaic. These tesserae would surely at their time of setting have been gilded!

I was fortunate to be traveling with a group of international mosaic experts, as part of the Fourth International Symposium on Turkish Mosaics, and sought out the Austrian scholar Veronika Scheibelreiter, an expert on evidential gold in mosaic floors, to show her of these extraordinary finds. She was ecstatic, and in confirming their origin, admitted to never having seen the evidence she had only known about…

# Experimenting & Enquiring

## Historical Viewpoints

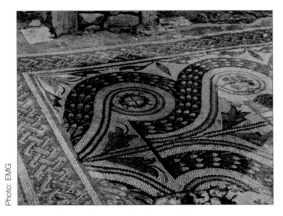

*Polychrome tesserae floor, detail, 3rd century, Dougga, Tunisia, constructed with local Numidian marble (bright orange/red/pink) from Chemtou*

It was, after all, an enquiry which from about the middle of the 3rd century BCE led the early mosaicists to change from using naturally-found pebbles in a design to choosing to seek for marble and stones to form tesserae – a material which was deliberately cut to a desired shape. This naturally gave greater manual and visual dexterity and a new medium was born.

These new-style tesserae could be used flat and given a smooth surface by grinding and waxing. They were also able to be made of colored materials and the fairly restrictive monochrome pebble palette gave way to floors which could be made of marbles from many countries, and even include semi-precious materials such as agate and onyx. Mosaic evolved as new materials and concepts were developed for the medium.

It was the annexing of Egypt by Rome in around 30 BCE which introduced glass and gold into mosaic. This resulted in the possibility of decorating new and variable surfaces in bright and polychrome color, which not only added rich textures and light but also necessitated a repositioning of the tesserae from smooth floor to an irregular wall surface, with all that this implied and still implies.

Not all change and experiment leads to a greater elaboration of the medium. One prime example of experimentation leading to a generally acknowledged decline grew out of the 16th century fashion of preserving paintings in mosaic. The great number of colors need to emulate painting was made possible by technical advances carried out in the Vatican workshops.

From 1572, when the Vatican workshop was established in Rome, there was a vast and ambitious scheme to mosaic much of the fabric of the basilica of St Peter, including the cupolas and

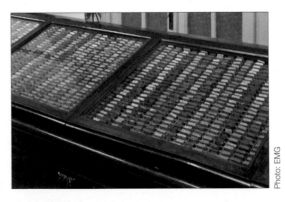

*The Vatican color sample cabinets, detail, Vatican City, Rome, Italy*

chapels, and even to replace the paintings.

For this, a great quantity of colored enamels or glass smalti was needed, and by experimenting with new mixes, eventually over 28,000 color examples were produced. The laboratory of mosaic which grew from this period onward is now called the Vatican Mosaic Studio.

In about 1775, a further experimental development occurred in the same laboratories when the *filati* technique was invented by Giacomo Rafaelli and Cesare Aguatti. This technique of spun enamel allowed the possibility of micro mosaic or miniature mosaic to evolve.

My visit in December 2006 to the Vatican studios enabled me to witness a continued flourishing of the miniature technique known as *smalti filati* – mosaics made up of cut threads of smalti-glass.

This invention opened other possibilities for the medium, and with the use of tiny tesserae, everyday objects and furniture could be embellished, e.g., jewelry boxes, pictures, and tables. Everybody wanted mosaic – and the style of miniature or micro mosaic was born, to allow the cultural elite who came on the Grand Tour to Rome, as well as devout pilgrims, to possess a souvenir from the Vatican. Even popes commissioned micro-mosaics for European Royalty.[1]

So popular was this mosaic style that until 1800 the Vatican Studio was one of the

---

[1] Pope Leo XIII gave Charles X an intricately-fashioned mosaic table in 1826.

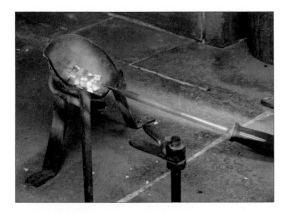

Heating a few glass smalti in a crucible.

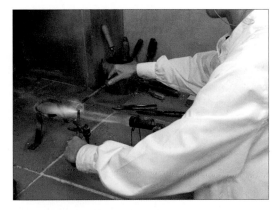

Applying direct heat from a gas burner

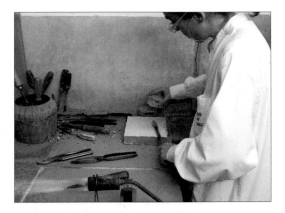

Flattening the molten glass before returning it to the heat

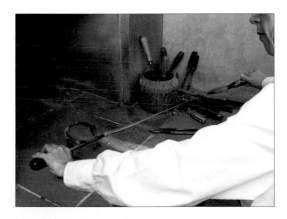

Stretching the molten glass between iron tweezers

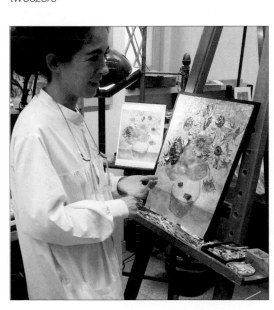

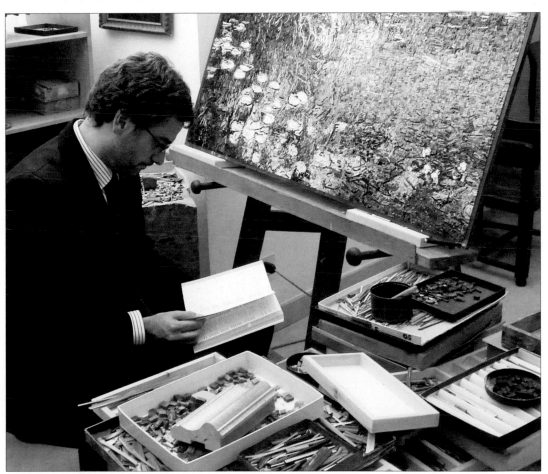

Left: The glass is cut from the thread of stretched glass, and used as tiny pinpoints of glass tesserae – note also the collection of variously-colored smalti filati.

Above: The Vatican Mosaic Workshop, detail, 2006. The Director, Paolo de Buona, creating a "picture for eternity" after the lily series of the French painter Claude Monet (1840-1926).

Photos: EMG

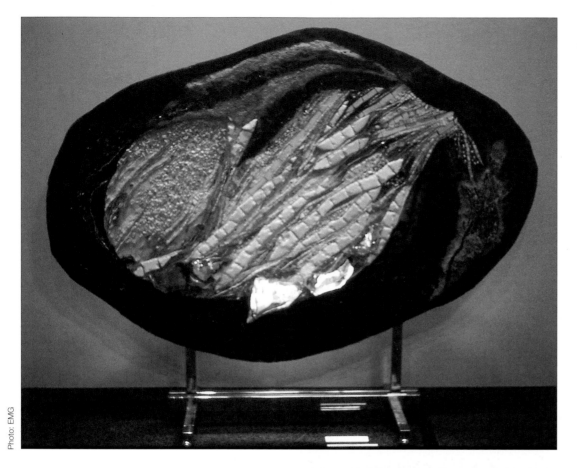

Photo: EMG

*Left:* Trasparenza*, 1984, Fernanda Tollemeto;*
*plexiglass, glass cullet*

*Below:* Ravenna 2007, *by Felice Nittolo,*
*52in x 51in x 116in /133cm x 130cm x 294cm*
*smalti*

largest-ever experimental mosaic laboratories.
The photographs on page 81 show *smalti filati*
being made at the furnace of the Studio of Mosaic
in 2006.

Nowadays the Vatican mosaic workshop
is run as a restoration studio and commissioning
studio, producing both secular and religious work.
It is exhilarating to know that specific artists today,
who use mosaic as their prime medium, are
experimenting with materials like plastic and fused
glass to give added meaning to their work. This
added flexibility, lightness and transparency is a far
cry from a medium traditionally known as one of
durability, strength and practicality.

The Italian artist Fernanda Tollemeto
(b. 1943) who works in Rome, has spent much of
her long and distinguished career experimenting

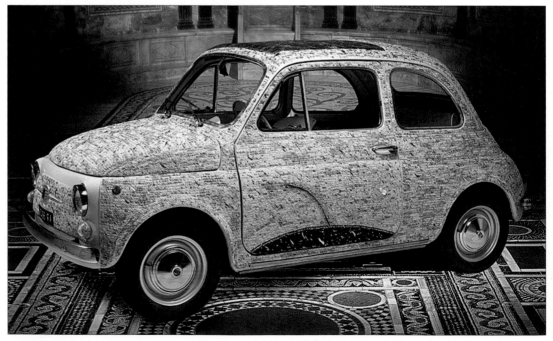

Photo: Roberto Morellini

within the medium in a search for absolute luminosity. Much of her work uses smalti and chunks of waste glass (cullet) embedded in and on translucent plexiglass for maximum transparency.

Other artists pushing the bounds of accepted meaning for the medium are France Hogué in Paris and Pascal Beauchamps (b. 1952) in Normandy in France, Hylya Ikizgül (b. 1966) in Istanbul, Turkey, and the Italians Nane Zavagno (b. 1932), and Giulio Candussio (b. 1945), in Friuli.

For the well-known artist Felice Nittolo (b. 1950) from Ravenna, Italy, mosaic shapes his whole personality. His work exudes light, color and above all a sense of the unexpected. An inveterate experimenter for the medium, he combines movement, plasticity, form and beauty in highly innovative ways, which are a synthesis of all that has been and possibly might be experienced through the mosaic medium.

By daring to experiment, new avenues for the medium are arrived at and the mosaic enquiry is kept open for the future. This, however, is often at the expense of the closed minds of Gallery owners, both nationally and provincially, who continue to see no further than tradition for the medium, allowing little truly contemporary mosaic work into their exhibition calendars.

# Inspirations from Contemporary Artists

The artists who illustrate this section are enquirers – forever moving the boundaries of mosaic making – through innovative techniques and application. Unable to accept the traditions alone, they explore deep into new territory, giving new and exciting directions for the medium.

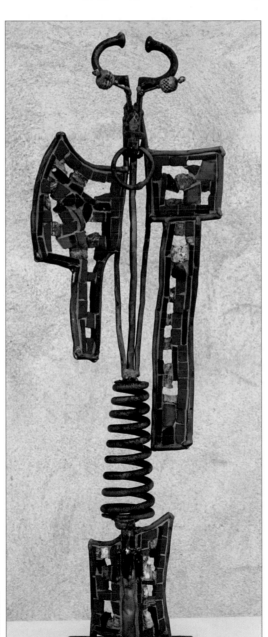

Photos: Gérard Brand

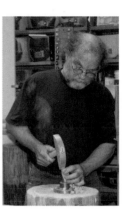

**Gérard Brand**
Born in Obernai, France in 1941.
Lives and works in Obernai, France.

I entitle my work *mosaïque autrement* [alterative mosaic making]. It is characterized not only by a specifically personal or contemporary artistic approach, but also, and mainly, by its relation to my everyday life – and this since early childhood! In my art I follow no fashion, no trends whatsoever.

For the work to be beautiful, it should above all be truthful. the harmony resulting from used materials.

***Parure de Fête***, 2006,
h. 27½in x w. 9½in x d.7in/ 70cm x 24cm x 18cm,
iron, marble, granite, glass paste

**Catherine Mandron**
Born in France, in 1938. Lives and works in La Celle St Cloud, Paris, France.

*Artist's Statement, Paris, France, 2007*
When I was a student at the Beaux Arts in Paris, France, I used to paint my sculptures. So my tutor sent me to Riccardo Licata's mosaic workshop. At that time no-one had ever incorporated mosaic into sculpture. Today, wanting to go further, I try to combine mosaic with wood and/or cement. The wood with its holes dictates the work and invites the spectator to look and turn the corners – I work in the spirit of the moment!

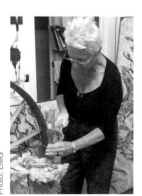
Photo: EMG

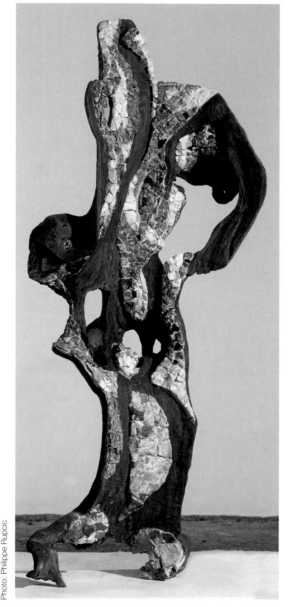
Photo: Philippe Rupcic

**L'Homme et la Tortue**, 2007, h. 75in/ 190cm, weathered wood, blue granite, pink, blue macao, yellow Naples, yellow marble, onyx, transparent/opaque glass paste

**Jan O'Highway**
Born in Henley-on-Thames, England, 1940. Lives and works in Totnes, England.

*Artist's Statement, Totnes, England, 2007*
Discarded plastic, broken toys, reactive glazes and fused glass on ceramic… the process of combining these characterful pieces into a mosaic is totally absorbing, a metaphor, perhaps, for the shattering and reconstruction of dreams.

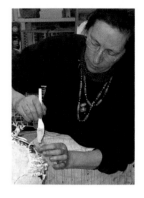

**Winter**, 2006, 12½in x 16½in / 32cm x 42cm; steel, resin, ceramic, plastic, toy parts, found materials.

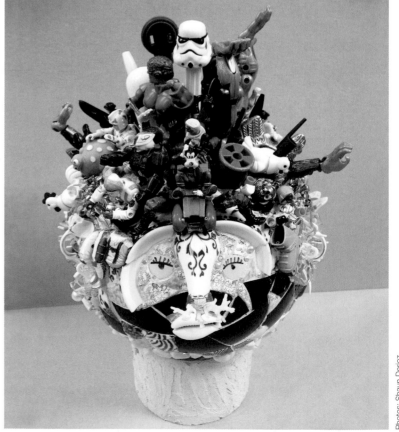
Photos: Shaun Derioz

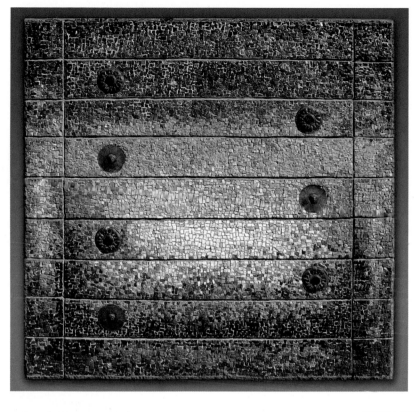

## George Trak

Born in Plovdiv, Bulgaria, 1961.   Lives and works in Plovdiv, Bulgaria.

*Artist's Statement, Plovdiv, Bulgaria, 2007*
My aim as an artist is to bring culture, art and economy together for both private and public art works.  I have a larger vision: for all Bulgarian Artists – to create an organization in Bulgaria for contemporary times, which will have a significant public role.

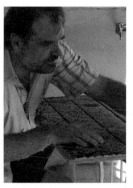

**Antakia**, 2007,
39½in x 39½in /100cm x 100cm;
smalti and metal inserts

Photos: George Trak

## Vanessa Somers Vreeland

Born in London, England, 1940s; lives and works in Rome, Italy, and in Marrakech, Morocco

*Artist's statement, Rome, Italy, 2006*
I am desperately figurative!  Shadows are so important – I just love light and shadow, the play between the two I've developed on my own in my tiny studio.  My work is inspired by the Roman technique.  If I get close to this I have succeeded but I work in totally different material, with lots of surprises, good surprises. The light bouncing off the glass makes you know it's glass and gives an intimacy and excitement which sucks you in – really exciting.

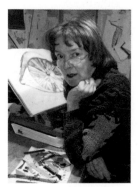

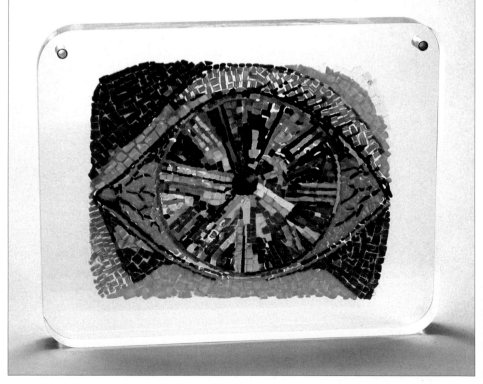

**Eye Wide Open**, 2007, 16in x 20in x 2in / 40cm x 50cm x 5cm, fused glass mosaic set in Perspex

Photos: Frederick Vreeland

# Communications 2007

## The Inspirational Mosaic

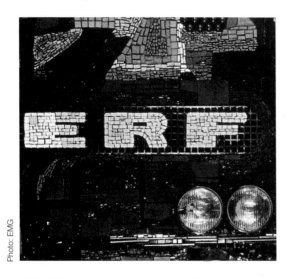

*Photo: EMG*

*ERF Vehicle Company, detail, by Hans Unger and Eberhard Schulze, 1966, smalti, tiles, enamel, miscellaneous parts (e.g., headlights), 41in x 95in /105cm x 240cm*

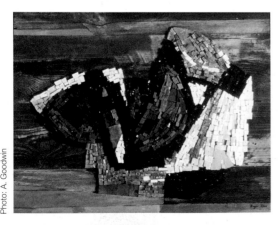

*Photo: A. Goodwin*

*Composition 1964, by Hans Unger, smalti, metallic gold tesserae on weathered wood, private collection*

## Background Revelations

I was first introduced to the work of Hans Unger (1915-1975) and his assistant Eberhard Schulze (b. 1938) by two of Unger's pupils, the German-born Hildegart Nicholas (1913-1995), considered his most inspired pupil, and Jane Muir (b.1929) a founder member of the AIMC. They both enthused – as do I – whenever encountering their work. Unger was one of the first mosaicists in the mid-20th century to realize new potentials for the medium, exploring abstract tendencies in the material and inserting *objets trouvés* and relevant miscellaneous objects, such as aluminum and copper, and vehicle or printing parts, to give added three-dimensional effects to enliven a mosaic surface still further – stunning!

Hans Unger was known in his lifetime as 'the Poster Artist', working memorably during the 1950s and 1960s for many companies in the United Kingdom, including London Transport, UNICEF, *Radio Times* (the BBC), and the Gas Board. However, in 1962 he began to experiment with mosaic, not only for posters but as an art form in its own right.

He had previously been to Italy in 1961, accompanied by his able assistant, Eberhard Schulze, to study mosaic-making and to view the mosaics of Venice, Florence and Ravenna, returning to London to make numerous mosaic posters for London Transport.

Unger reveled in the subtlety of color combinations obtainable in mosaic, sometimes setting colors next to each other to set up scintillating visual vibrations. But it was effects of light on tesserae which excited him most – and for this he began to set the tesserae at differing heights from the picture plane, to create nuances of shade and light.

Whereas historically a smooth surface was a *desideratum* of mosaic, Unger began to work with other materials alongside the tesserae, e.g., wood, slate, metals and ceramic, to give heightened textural contrasts.

With the traditional narrative element no longer necessary for him, the abstract qualities of the medium could come to the fore, and even if Unger might have started with recollection – of a landscape or other form – when beginning a new work, it was his spontaneous manipulation of the material which took precedence, a way of launching mosaic into an exciting future.

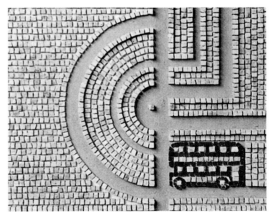

*Photo: EMG*

*Busabout (detail) by Hans Unger and Eberhard Schulze, 1972, ungrouted white marble and red smalti, c. 30in x 36in / 76cm x 92cm, London Transport Museum, London, UK*

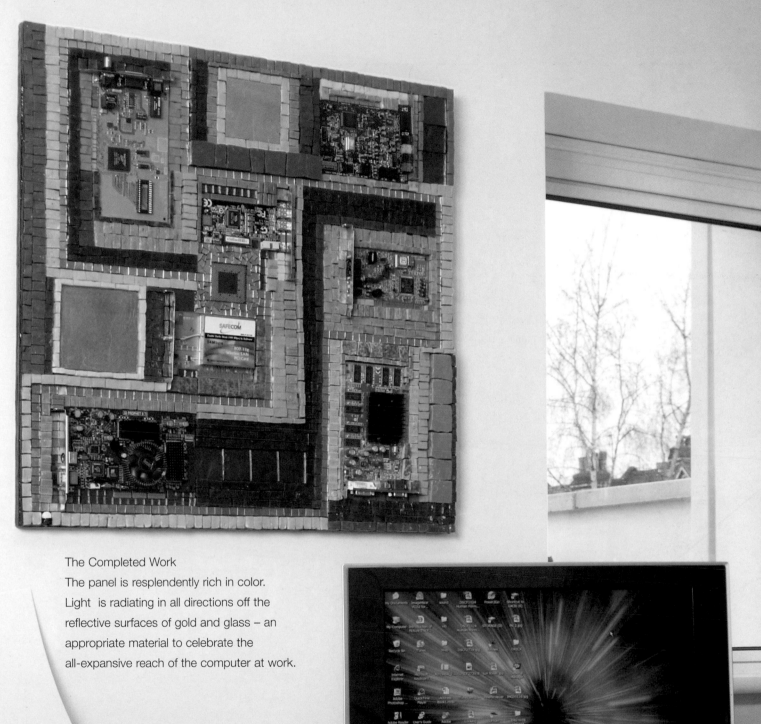

The Completed Work

The panel is resplendently rich in color.
Light is radiating in all directions off the
reflective surfaces of gold and glass – an
appropriate material to celebrate the
all-expansive reach of the computer at work.

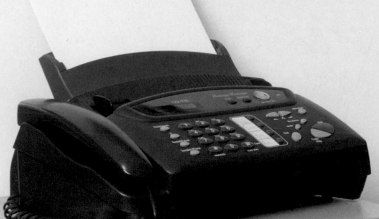

## Method

### Concerning the design

The inspiration for the work came from communicating by email with my younger musician son Darius throughout 2007. At first he was resident in Tokyo, Japan, in the east, but towards the end of the year he was performing jazz piano on a cruise ship, frequently docking at New York, America, in the west. As all parents are aware, this necessary power of communication is both daunting and miraculous.

### Equipment and Materials

½in / 12mm plywood, 24in x 24in / 61cm x 61cm

gold ink

brush

pencil

ruler or steel rule

2-component epoxy adhesive

plastic spatula

pva/white glue

container

palette knife

colored ink/pigment of choice

mosaic nippers

a palette of variously sized smalti in turquoise
    greens, greens and yellows

Venetian gold leaf or metallic glazed tiles

table easel (optional)

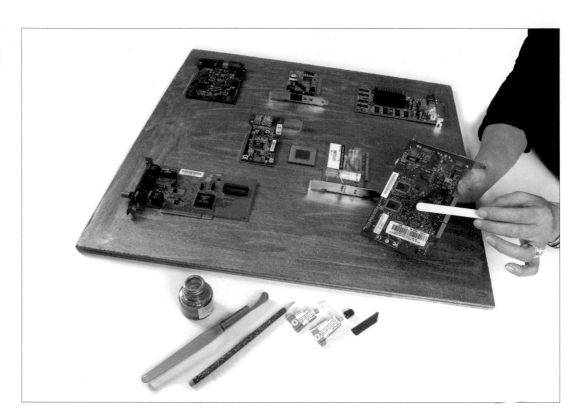

### The Drawing

For this work the materials will take the lead – the computer parts and the smalti – on a board with equal sides. There is no drawing as such – just my direct response to the given title *Communications 2007* – and an attempt to create a work in which the design and the mosaic material are mutually dependent.

1 The board was primed with a coating of gold ink, applied by brush to ensure any exposed surface reflected this metallic finish and not the timber surface.

Take time assembling any miscellaneous objects; a 'natural' positioning seems to occur, where balance and aesthetic value with reference to shape and color or texture seems to happen. When happy with the placement, use the epoxy adhesive to fix the components to the board.

Because the surfaces of the computer parts were uneven, it was easier to mix equal quantities of each component on the back of each part and allow the mix to set before placing in the required position.

Epoxy glue is a wonderful adhesive, able to bond metal, glass, plastic, ceramic, wood or rubber. Certain procedures must be followed. For example:

1. the surfaces to be stuck together must be dry and clean
2. equal quantities of both the hardener and the resin must be used at each application
3. all the surfaces need to set before bonding together (read the manufacturer's instructions)
4. the tubes should be stored in a dry temperate place.
5. follow maximum safety procedures at all times.

The rest of the work will use pva or white glue to secure the more traditional materials, with just a little coloring added to the adhesive at the time of mixing.

Use the pencil and ruler to help create a labyrinthine path around the computer parts – straight and precise lines seemed preferable to any organically drawn pathway for this design.

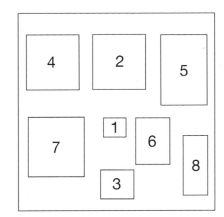

The diagram shows the computer parts used in the mosaic

1. processor (from a motherboard)
2. USB (universal serial bus) card
3. wireless LAN (local area network)
4. network Ethernet card
5. sound blaster line card
6. modem
7. graphics card
8. monitor

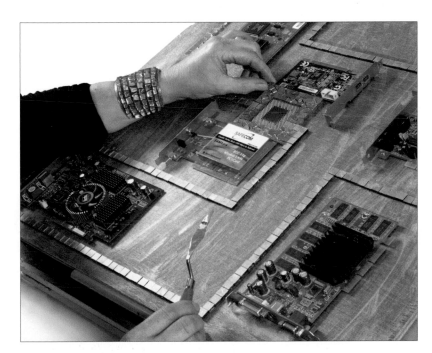

2 Use regularly-cut squares of gold or bright colored glazed tiles to form the "pathway of light" linking each component. In this early stage, the design should have a fairly balanced quality.

A strong golden center was added at this point at the center of the pathway to stabilize it and give it an end and a beginning.

3 A palette of various turquoise greens, green and yellow smalti and Venetian gold leaf. The colors chosen for this work are a palette of wonderful variants of green, turquoise green and yellow. These allude to the "communication" referred to in the title of the work – e-mails from the ether via land, sea and sky.

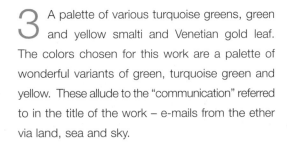

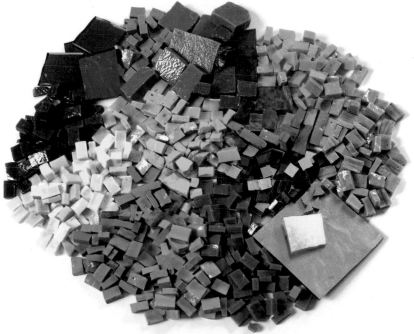

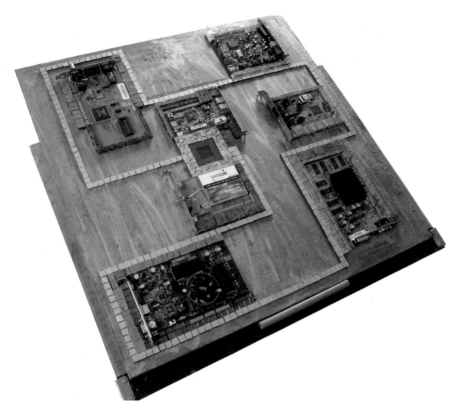

4 To be sure of linking each computer part to the design as a whole, smalti, of a color corresponding to the part, was used to surround each computer component. The nature of smalti, a Venetian handmade mosaic glass, is always somewhat irregular in shape, size, coloration or consistency – use these idiosyncrasies to advantage, sometimes laying the tesserae flat, on edge, or as large chunks.

When creating a mosaic in this way, as an abstract, concerned with color, texture, form and weight, i.e., the balance of the design as a whole, it is advisable to work at an angle, either by propping the backing board on a piece of wood or other object to tilt the work at a slight angle, or by using a table easel, which can be adjusted at will.

5 Work on the central area of the panel in rich yellows and olive green. The deep rich yellow smalti makes a startling contrast to the upside down Venetian gold leaf glass, where the brilliant turquoise backing glass allows the metal to glow through it in strong shimmering tones. Much of the color build-up is instinctive, but be aware of contrasting tones and hues – light against dark and juxtapose the complementary shades.

Keep surface texture in mind too: juggle the heights, size and shape of the tesserae to build up a complex and heady mix of all three. I have added two plates of gold leaf, partly to enhance the design by adding a smooth expanse of one color and to give two large elements of reflective light, in marked contrast with the visual intimacies of the computer parts.

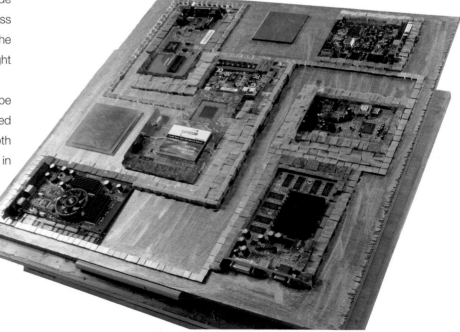

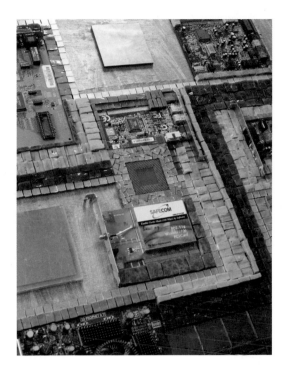

6 Build up the design – by eye and intuition. Add rich contrasting tones of deep turquoise greens. Although this style of working is instinctive – by looking and assessing – pay attention to the visual "weight" of the panel – the overall balance.

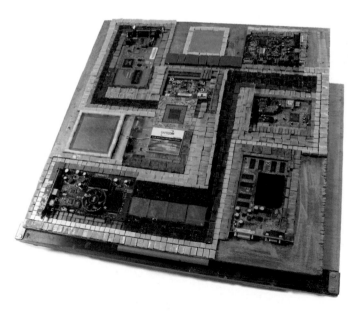

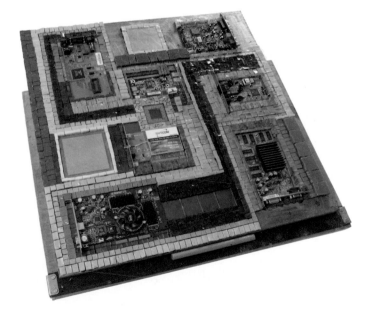

7 Continue to build up the design with the Venetian smalti, enjoying the variants of color and size. The work is contained within a square shape – there is no need to emphasize one area over another, and there is no ultimate focal point, no area or place to aspire to – the eye should move easily from one area to another with equal interest.

8 Take special care in color-balancing the design. Stand back from the design from time to time to survey the overall effect of the work – to find balance and pleasing aesthetic placing. This may sound very remote and esoteric, but with looking, and trusting your own eye and sensibility to this most illustrious of mosaic materials, you will find the design creates its own visual momentum.

# Windows

## Inspiration

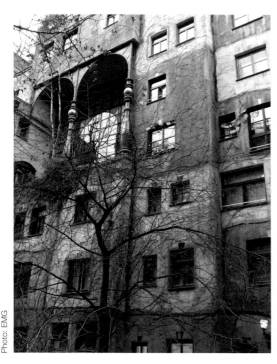

Photo: EMG

*Windows*, Das Kunsthaus *(The Art House),*
*Vienna, 1991, by Friedensreich Hundertwasser,*
*Vienna, Austria*

The Completed Work
The mosaic in position on the terrace of Dar
Aicha adds rich color, fun and a surreal touch,
elements so beloved of Hundertwasser, and
exaggerated by the glorious light of this extreme
north-western part of Africa, where the sun or
candlelight can turn the ordinary and everyday
into fantastical living theatre.

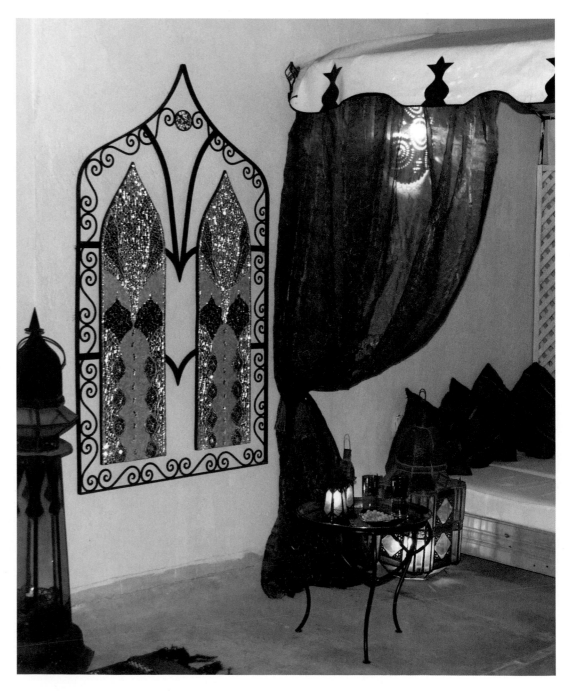

# Background Revelations

It was only in January 2007 that I saw for myself the buildings of Friedensreich Hundertwasser (1928-2000) in Vienna and experienced the full impact of his work. On a gloomy wet and cold day his buildings of color and reflected light were more human in scale than I had imagined, more approachable and full of FUN! It is rare to experience architecture as 'laugh-aloud joyous' – I needed to know more...

The windows in particular caught my attention – each played a role in the building's façade, being either surrounded by bright color or acquiring mosaic sills of colorful free formation glazed ceramic tiles on slightly irregular surfaces which sparkled at various incidences of light.

Friedensreich (Stowasser) Hundertwasser, architect, painter, ecologist and philosopher, was a Viennese. After attending the Academy of Fine Arts in Vienna for three months and the Ecole des Beaux Arts in Paris for only one day, he began traveling extensively, spending the spring and winter of 1951 in Marrakech and other cities of Morocco. Color intrigued him – the green roofs (green being an Islamic holy color) were for Hundertwasser a revelation, and he is quoted as saying "For a house, grass is the natural roofing".

Early in the 1950s he wrote manifestos against rationalism in architecture, deploring the straight line as being the only uncreative line.

Many of his buildings seem invariably to be defined by their windows. For Hundertwasser (as for many an artist) the windows are equivalent to the eyes, and as such, form a connection between an inside and an outside. From this basic tenet he developed a life philosophy. In 1958 he demanded a *Fensterrecht* – a 'window right' – for all; this demanded that each resident had the freedom to recreate the area outside his window - an area within the reach of a brush. Residents too should be given the freedom to re-create this space for themselves, thus recognizing that they were creating living windows which should give pleasure as well as allowing an outsider to observe and think "there lives a human being."

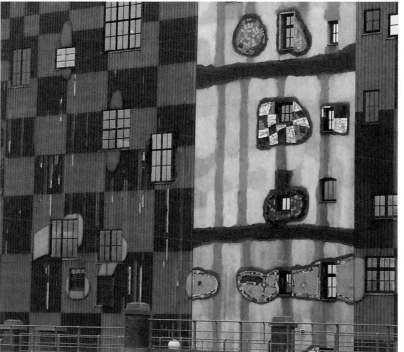

Houses with Green Roofs and Gardens, *Marrakech, (detail) by Friedensreich Hundertwasser, 1953*

*Windows (detail), Spittelau District Heating Plant (Fernwärme building), Vienna, Austria, by Friedensreich Hundertwasser, 1988-91*

Photo: EMG

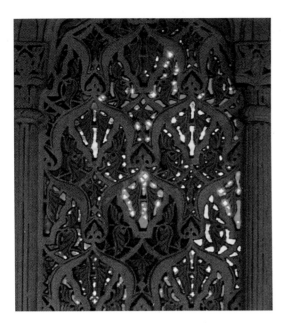

*Detail, small* chemmassiat *window, mosque of the Muhammad V Mausoleum, Rabat, Morocco*

## Concerning the Form

Building on Hundertwasser's idea of personalizing a window space – even in creating a window where there was none! – provides inspiration for my design. It comes from the Moroccan tradition of the 'false' *chemmassiat*. These are arched window shapes, often grouped in threes, of geometric or ornamental designs made in a beautiful lacework of plaster (called *gebs*), known since the 14th century. The plaster is of the very palest pink in Marrakech, but it can be tinted when it is mixed, and before the intricate carving begins. These false windows are used to great decorative effect high up in a building or above doors.

I wanted to introduce a window into my studio-home *Dar Aicha* in Marrakech. It is a traditional *riad* – a courtyard home with no visible windows on the outside. I wanted to give the home an inner eye, to let in light and fun – what better place than a sun-drenched terrace.

**Secret Insight 2**
The word *chemmassiat* is derived from the Arabic word *chems*, meaning 'sun'. Originally these windows had a completely pierced plaster surround – the technique known as *gebs* in Moroccan – into which pieces of colored glass in brilliant reds, yellow, green and blue are fitted to allow the sunlight to pass through, creating isolated pinpoints of rich colored light within. Gorgeous!

# Method

## The Drawing

**1** The drawing is one of free form – repeated on two arched window forms (Hundertwasser's loathing of the straight line or ruler forbade me from using it except to find a central line from which to work).

## Materials

2 arch-shaped boards of
  exterior plywood, 39 x 14in/
  100 x 36cm
A4 sheet of black card
red felt-tipped marker
scissors
ruler        brush
gold ink     pencils

The sheet of black card was bent in half and a random 'V' shape cut, which tapered from its top to the bottom. When opened out, this shape was placed on each of the two backing boards and its pencil outline drawn. This drawing was firmed up with the marker pen. Irregularly-drawn tessera-shaped pieces were also added from the lower edge of the cut shapes to the base of the board. The gold ink was used to brush-infill the outlined area.

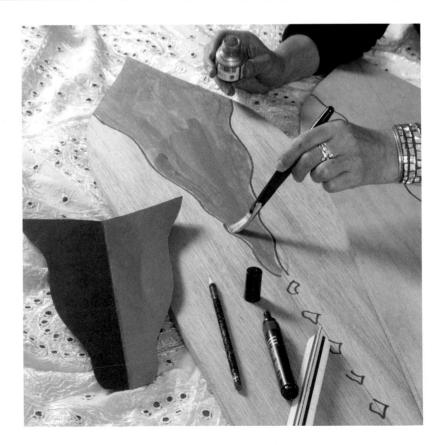

## Interpretation and Technique

All the materials in this mosaic will be glass and will reflect light to varying degrees, dependent on their surface mirror qualities, to produce a surface which will bounce light to and fro, not through – as plate glass windows do – to create a window of reflecting and refractive light.

## Materials

silver-backed mirror and mirror glass,
opaque stained glass
*smalti* or vitreous mosaic tiles in colors
 of reds, yellow; and rich yellow gold
Venetian colored gold
wheeled nippers
white glue/pva adhesive

containers
palette knives
golden ink/pigment to color
 the adhesive
prodder
sealer

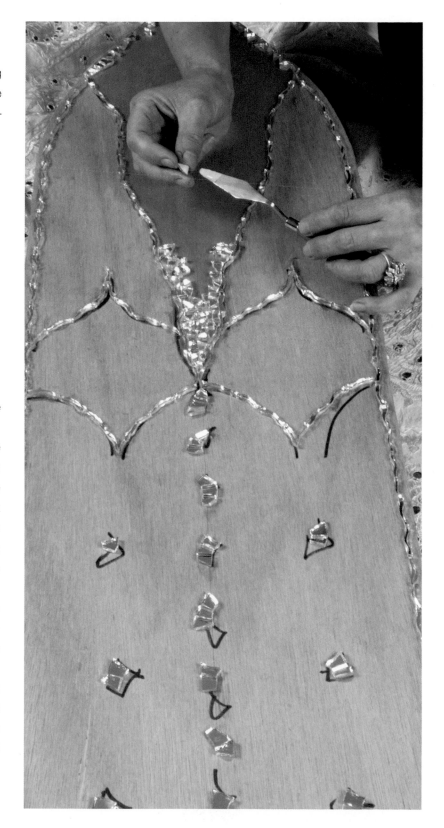

2   Begin filling in the "V"-shaped area with irregular cut mirror tesserae using a random crazy paving technique (*opus palladianum*).

Use an adhesive mixed with golden pigment to glue the mirror to the timber base. This has the effect of glowing through the interstices between the tesserae. The mirror tesserae should vary somewhat in size as they move towards the upper edge – becoming steadily larger in shape. Below the apex of the 'V'-like form, add small concentrated areas of mirror in groups of two or three tesserae in a downward line (this may mean ignoring the positioning of the initially drawn groupings of the under-drawing). On each side of this central line add a similar line of small loosely-spaced groups of mirror.

The two long arched shapes are edged with thin ribbons of undulating mirror, leaving up to ¼in / 1cm from the edge clear. Outline also the freely-drawn shape – an inverted V-like form, which visually "lets in light" – with further cut ribbons of curved mirror tesserae.

Outline these two outer groupings with undulating ribbons of tesserae in a rich golden stained glass, forming arabesque-like shapes around each small grouping of mirror. Using a yellow mirror glass, outline a fan-like form away from the central random shape, and begin to fill in with rich red Venetian gold.

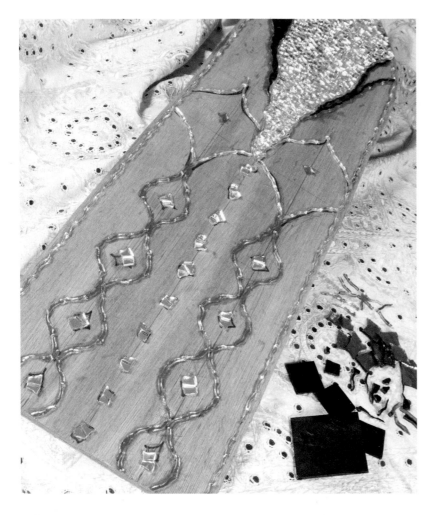

3 Using the rich golden glass, fill in the areas on either side of the V-shaped apex, introducing a small golden center-piece cut in a loose square shape. Cut more golden arabesque shapes from the yellow gold mirror glass, and create additional fan-shaped divisions at the top part of each mosaic, using the same material. Use the Venetian gold to edge the mosaic, taking care to follow the shape of the undulating ribbon slivers.

Into this basic form now comes brilliant color – so beloved of Hundertwasser and the Moroccans. Within each arabesque form cut bright red smalti or vitreous glass and fill each eye-shaped section.

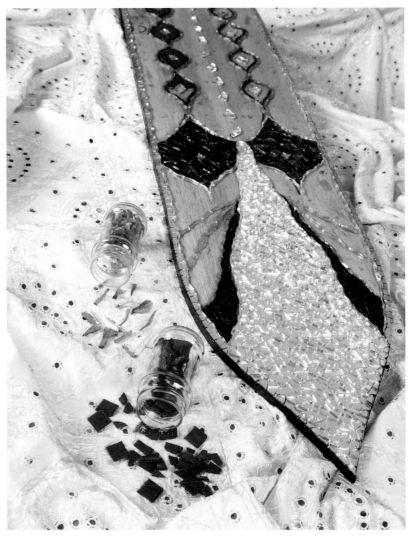

4 Use the same or another strong red smalti or vitreous glass to fill in a second fan-like division. A vibrant yellow glass, very opaque with delicious color-mixing 'faults' is used to fill in various areas of the mosaic to give a bright ground. The prodder becomes an excellent tool for positioning awkward shapes.

### Secret Insight 3
The *arabesque* originated from spirals and is essentially an organic form. It is a term used to refer to Islamic decoration which is derived from ancient plant-like scroll designs or vegetal motifs, e.g., stems, buds, flowers and leaves. It can also be used visually as a metaphor for life. It is not a mechanical form but is a flowing line, continuous and intertwining but with a hidden order. Because the curves are never mechanically drawn, they give a dynamic, if uncertain, quality to a design.

**5** Introduce strong yellows to enrich the design still further. The remainder of the works are finished using *opus palladianum* in standard silver-backed mirror glass.

## Concerning *Opus Palladianum*

This way of laying a background may look simple, but it is a highly refined technique and an excellent one for filling in areas of a mosaic which have no clearly defined form. The nature of crazy paving depends, for its best outcome in mosaic, on superb tessellation, i.e., cutting which takes into account the shapes of all the tesserae which surround each individual piece. For truest effect, it depends on scrutinizing each area to be filled with a sensitive empathy towards its neighboring pieces.

## Grouting and Hanging

## Materials

| | |
|---|---|
| white Portland cement | water |
| gold permanent pigment / ink | cloths |
| containers | polishing cloth |
| protective gloves | metal frame |
| small trowel | |

Put a quantity of white Portland cement into a container and add a sufficient quantity of gold ink or pigment to give a rich color to the grout, adding extra water if needed, and form a thickish mortar. Wearing gloves, rub this into the surface of both mosaics, taking great care around the narrow ribbon mirror tesserae as these may have sharp cutting edges. When well grouted, wipe clean and leave to cure under damp cloths for three days. Clean with quantities of cold water.

## Framing

The two arched forms were inserted into a frame which echoes a traditional arabesque shape. It was made for me by the local metal workers from the *Souk Haddadine* (blacksmiths' market), for which Marrakech is famed. The design was drawn by me in the morning and made by the evening of the next day – with an added central circular element which was duly filled with mirror mosaic.

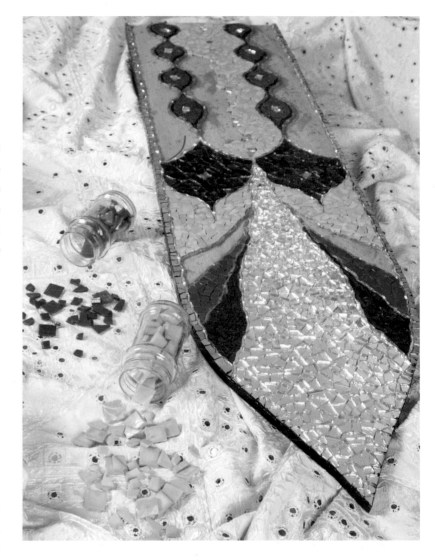

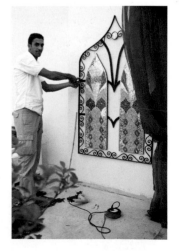

Samir, my charming and practical house manager kindly hung the work in its position on the terrace wall.

# Ceiling Rose

## The Inspirational Mosaic

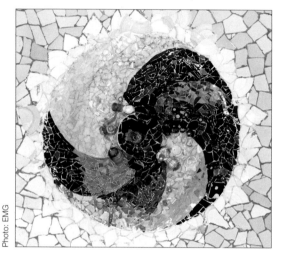

Photo: EMG

*Ceiling rose, detail (1910-1913), by J M Jujol, from the Hall of a Hundred Columns, Parc Güell, Barcelona, Spain*

## Background Revelations

Looking upwards in the Hall of a Hundred Columns, or Hypostyle Hall designed by Antoni Gaudì, is arresting – rosettes made up of a wondrous ensemble of color and texture greet the eye. These are by Gaudì's extraordinarily visionary apprentice, Josep Maria Jujol (1879-1949), who was given free rein by his great master to explore his creative expressiveness.

Jujol uses not only white *trencadis* (mosaic made up of discarded factory china and tiles and glass) as an overall ceiling skin in the Hall, but where columns have been left out – columns which in themselves seem to flout gravity – he has

created collage-like rosettes of broken plates, glass bottles, and even dolls' faces, to make powerful and expressive abstract compositions.

This dramatic space was constructed between 1903 and 1910 in the Güell Park as a market place. In reality the '100 columns' are only 86 in number. They are hollow and act as channels, taking the rain water from the Serpentine Bench above to a water cistern below, and out through the mouth of the well-known huge, polychrome mosaic lizard.

This interconnecting architectural marvel was an ambitious project made possible by Gaudì's great patron Eusebi Güell who, it is said, took inspiration for this innovative park from the English Garden City.

The Catalan architect Jujol was only 27 years old when he met Gaudì, with whom he worked until the latter's death. His memorable

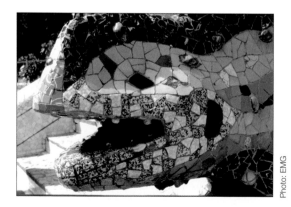

Photo: EMG

*Lizard fountain, detail, by A. Gaudì, Parc Güell, Barcelona, Spain. Water is channeled through the creature, with the mouth acting as a fountain spout*

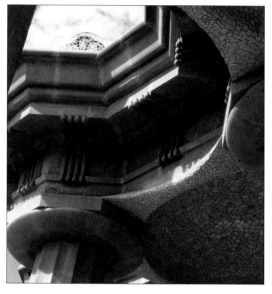

Photo: EMG

*Hall of a Hundred Columns, 1910-1913, design A. Gaudì (note on the top a glimpse of part of the Serpentine Bench), Parc Güell, Barcelona, Spain*

decorative 'skin' on Gaudì's sculptural architecture is highly revolutionary, pre-dating even Pablo Picasso's innovative collage work.

The ceiling of the Hypostyle Hall is itself a richly expressive form, its light and shadow made more emphatic with its white coating of *opus paladianum* mosaic work. The large, colorful, star-like rosettes and smaller, more delicate ceiling roses with spiral forms occur where there are no columns, and heighten the sense of lost or missing columns. The richly-patterned compositions, whose materials include some distinctly blue perfume bottles, astound, intrigue and delight by their absurd beauty – fore-runner to the Dada movement.

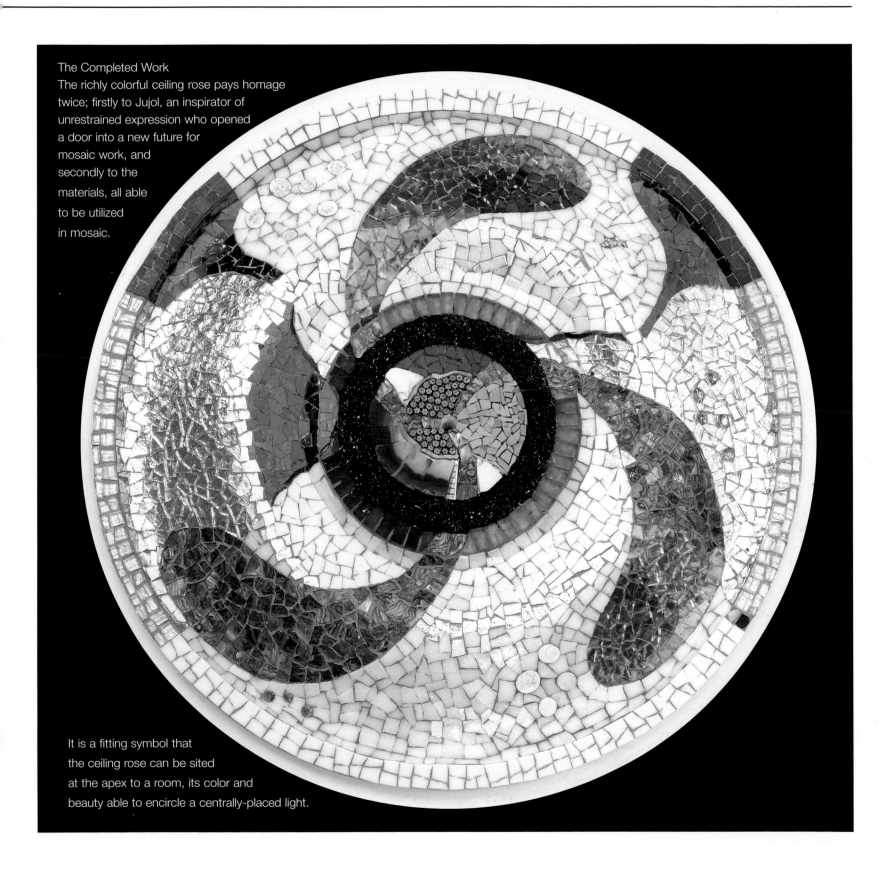

The Completed Work
The richly colorful ceiling rose pays homage twice; firstly to Jujol, an inspirator of unrestrained expression who opened a door into a new future for mosaic work, and secondly to the materials, all able to be utilized in mosaic.

It is a fitting symbol that the ceiling rose can be sited at the apex to a room, its color and beauty able to encircle a centrally-placed light.

## Method

### Concerning the Materials

Jujol was a spontaneous creator. He was truly innovatory in using discarded materials in his work, e.g., rubbished pottery and glass, and the waste ceramic materials from tile firms. He used these materials out of context, without their designated purpose, simply for the lavish delight of their texture, color or inimitable surface properties.

All the materials used in this work are ones that can, and have been used in mosaic making. They are both enduring and have unique characters of their own. I wanted the work to celebrate the rich variety of each of the materials, jostling together for attention.

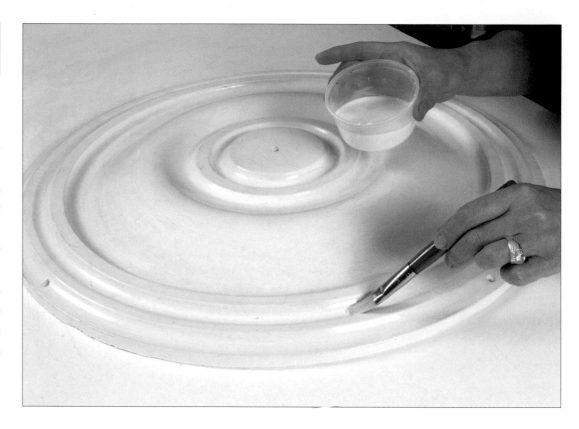

### Materials and Equipment

plaster ceiling rose
electric drill and bit
brush
container
marker pen
a miscellany of materials including;
 *millefiori,* mirror glass, abalone shells
mother of pearl
hologram jewelry
stained glass

smalti
flat shells
Venetian gold leaf
decorative gravel
pva/white glue
mosaic nippers (and electric jig-saw – optional)
palette
knife
small brush
tweezers

1 The plaster ceiling rose was first drilled to create the hanging holes, and then primed with diluted white glue/pva to give a secure bonding surface on which to work. The adhesive was greatly diluted at least 50/50, and brushed over the whole area in two coats, allowing a drying time between each coating.

---

**Secret Insight 1**

Many an artist has taken inspiration from the innovatory mosaic/collage work of Jujol. In Spain, artists Pablo Picasso (1881-1973), Joan Miró (1893-1983), Salvador Dali (1904-1989); and Antonì Tapies (b.1923 ); and worldwide Niki de St Phalle (1930-2002), Friedenreich Hundertwasser (1928-2000), Julian Schnabel (b.1951), and the author.

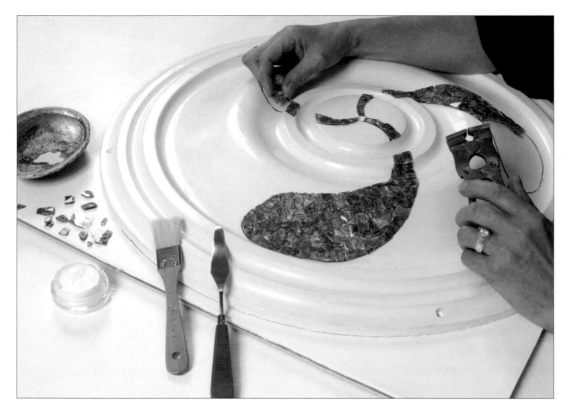

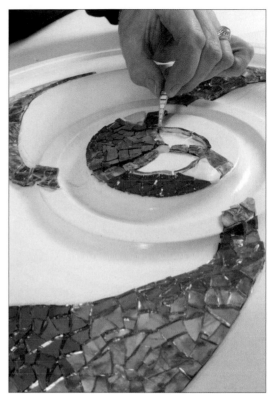

2 I felt the spiral form Jujol introduced into his ceiling roses (he also used a star shape) was a great one for giving movement and energy to the design. A very simple design using this concept was drawn onto the ceiling rose using a permanent marker.

Abalone shells were then cut and applied in thin layers to begin the design. The shell was cut using both the saw and the mosaic cutters.

The nature of this way of working – i.e., with miscellaneous objects – involves personal choices and availability of materials. As always in mosaic, choose materials which you have an affinity with, for whatever reason, and work with these, building up areas of color, texture and height, which complement each other, yet which vie for attention.

Brightly colored stained glass and mirror glass were cut to infill the shapes formed by the spiral form; the strong warm orange colors scintil-latingly vibrate against their opposing colors – the greens and turquoises of the abalone shell. The mirror uses *opus palladianum*, cut quite small and tightly tessellated to give a multi-facetted surface to encounter any light falling on the curving surface of the plaster rose. This opus comes into its own when working on undulating surfaces, collecting and dispersing light in many directions.

The rich surface of orange-colored Venetian gold leaf is used for greatest effect in the central part where very small tessarae form a dense area of color. Individual tesserae of mother of pearl, larger in size, also add their soft nacreous light in the design build up.

3 A piece of jewelry was also added, its hologram finish adding another enriching touch. Tiny roundels of millefiori were then added, using tweezers to position them, in two separate sections.

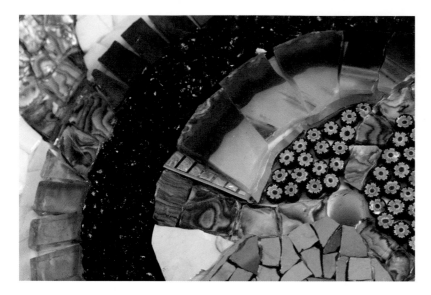

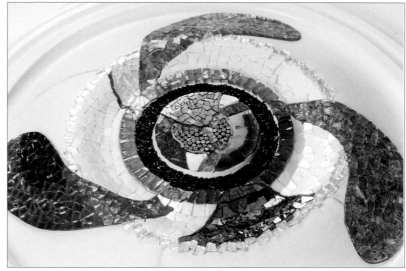

4   The inner circle was completed with agate in a rich russet brown color. The agate was cut quite easily using the mosaic nippers. The gap surrounding this area was filled with glass frit, a material which can be used to great advantage in mosaic, adding a textured surface reflecting pinpoints of light. This was surrounded with trasparenti smalti, again in warm orange hues.

5   As in the ceiling rosettes created by Jujol, much of the remaining area will be filled with white or light-colored materials, giving a light-colored surrounding – a good background to allow all the materials to compete for attention. Even here, though, introduce some occasional strong color and surface variants, e.g., tesserae with a luster finish, to give oblique highlights.

Continue working around the center in a white vitreous glass with a luster finish. Work within an edge of silvered mirror glass put as a randomly-placed line on the crest of the curve of the roundel to accentuate reflective interest. Introduce a deep green luster stained glass, added for its color contrast with the intense bright orange glass.

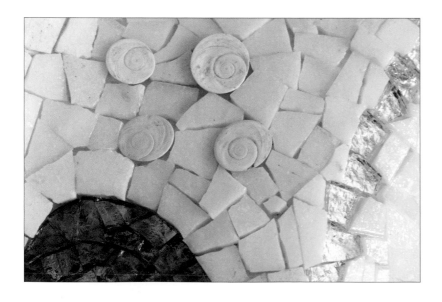

6   The remaining area is completed in white vitreous glass using *opus palladianum*. Other inserts are added into this; a small silver lizard, a few decorative gems, and some shells – a favorite mosaicist's material. These were fairly flat fossilized shells found on a visit to Australia – an artist of mosaic is like a magpie, forever on the alert, forever lured to pick up new and exciting materials to add to a collection for future use.

The ceiling rose was edged with manufactured vitreous tiles. Full use was made of their bevelled edges, which formed a tight joint to both seal and frame the circular mosaic. Each edging color corresponded with the color it joined up to. The transparent vitreous tiles were "silvered" by glueing aluminum leaf to their backs before being cut and applied – a technique which can be used with any transparent glass.

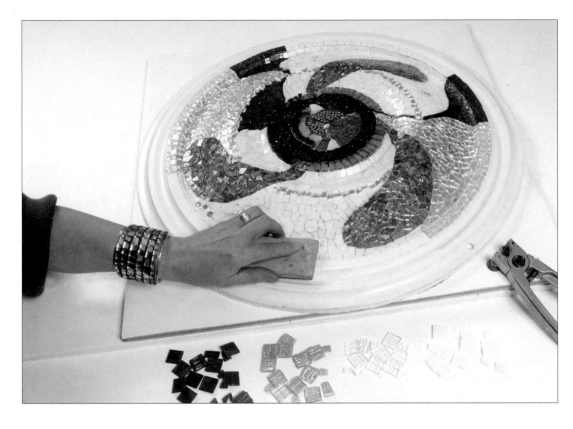

7 The edge was first smoothed, using a fine diamond file to level any uneven edges, before the bevel-edged vitreous tesserae were applied. It is advisable to use a dust-mask for this procedure.

## Grouting

## Materials

| | | |
|---|---|---|
| a proprietary gray grout | protective gloves | cloths |
| bowls/containers | small trowel | water |

8 The outer area only of the mosaic will be grouted. Grouting the inner area may detract from the clarity of the colors if cement should lodge in their intricate surface parts.

Wear protective gloves and mix a quantity, about 2 cupfuls, of a proprietary gray grout with water to form a stiff mortar. Carefully grout the outer areas of the ceiling rose. Clean, and leave for 2 to 3 days under damp cloths before carefully washing with clean water.

If desired, fix the mosaic in position on the ceiling, allowing an upward-facing pendant light to hang from the center to give maximum interest. If preferred, the work could also be hung on a wall.

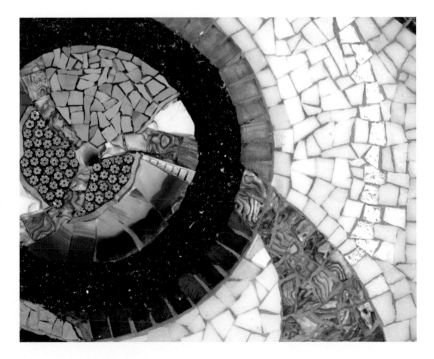

# The Spire

## Inspiration

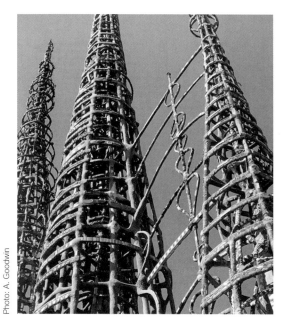

Watts Tower, *1921-1955, detail, by Simon Rodia, Los Angeles, California, USA*

The Completed Work

The Spire, *Princesshay, Exeter, 2008.* Note the Roman/mediaeval wall in the foreground and the ancient 11th century cathedral of Exeter in the central far distance.

     The tiny tesserae of the spire reflect the constant rhythm of 21st century urban life as a movement of light, held in an aspiring form – a great symbol for an upwardly mobile city. The tesserae reflect the capricious nature of light, except for one stone tessera – a Roman one – whose constancy is there to hint at the city's Roman past, when, as one of England's earliest Roman settlements in the 1st century AD, it was known as *Isca Dumnoniorum*.

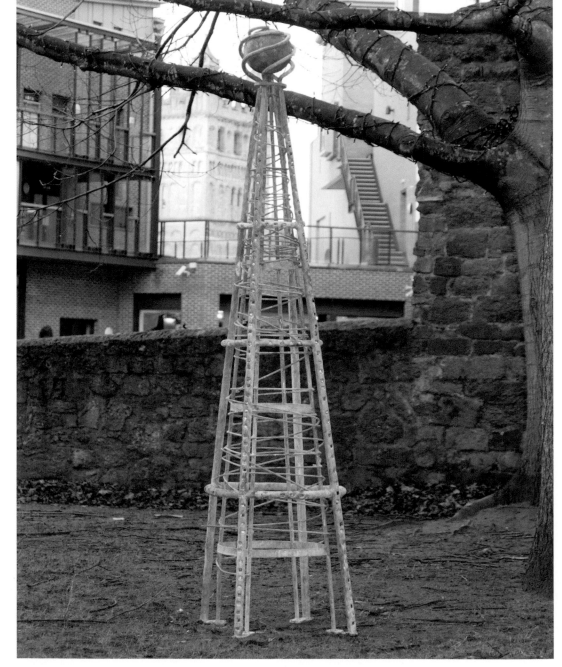

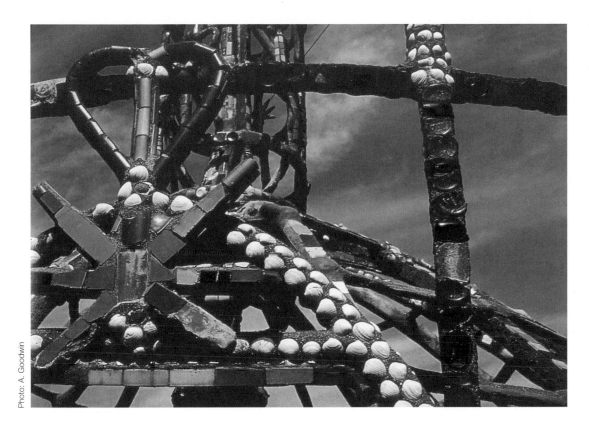

Photo: A. Goodwin

Watts Towers, *detail, showing the application of ceramic, tiles, shells, glass bottles, and miscellaneous ornaments*

## Background Revelations

I have not, as yet, seen for myself the Watts Towers, but those of my close acquaintances who have, have relayed back to me their experience of them, with effusive enthusiasm at this singular man's artistic achievement... and I am inspired.

The three main towers are part of an extraordinary work of art which spanned 34 years of making. Their creator was an Italian immigrant to the USA known as Simon Rodia (1879-1965), a tile maker and cement worker by trade. Within a small triangular area of land in an outlying area of Los Angeles, he created a group of 17 sculptures, the most memorable part of which includes three towering spires, known as the West, Central and Eastern towers. They rise up to a height of almost 100ft/ 30m, and are constructed using a scrap steel armature. This was then covered in steel wire, wire mesh and cement, the steel acting as a cement reinforcement. The whole was then decorated; sometimes with china and tile in an array of bright color combinations, or faced with white shells and bric-a-brac.

The work is a marvel on two main counts; first as a complex engineering feat – the towers were constructed in situ, acting themselves as a scaffolding of small-spanned walkways and arches; and secondly as an inspirational structure of poignant beauty – it was made alone by an untutored visionary man, a solitary artist with a driving passion.

The artist's wonderful aesthetic sense is apparent in the structure as a whole and in the masterly putting together of the materials. Rodia has created in effect an enormous 3D mosaic, not begun until he was 42 years of age, and then without machines or drawings – merely artistic experimentation and conviction.

### Secret Insight I

Simon Rodia's desire to build something big, even monumental, may well have arisen from childhood memories when, as a young boy in the province of Avellino in Southern Italy, he would have viewed huge portable towers of wood and paper being carried in the streets as part of an annual summer festival parade.

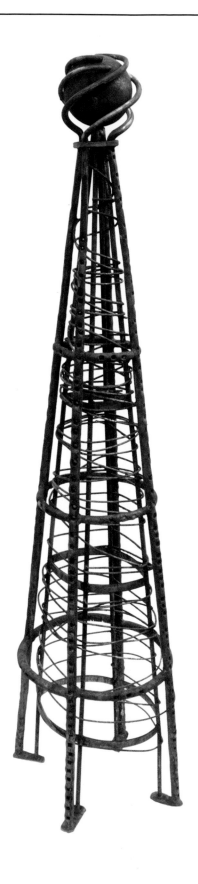

## Concerning the Form

The spire is a free-standing metal sculpture, with a cannon-ball finial, and is constructed with galvanized steel and the overall dimensions are 78½in x 22in / 200cm x 56cm. The original design concept is the author's, the base structure is by Les Clifton and additional steel elements were made by metal sculptor Richard Bent. Richard, who was himself inspired by the works of Rodia, created the inner spiral form as a compliment the original towers in both structural and conceptual complexity.

---

**Secret Insight 2**

The materials of the Watts Towers are a rich repository of tiles, glass and pottery. The manufactured tiles and bottle-glass ware bears witness to a time of domestic utilitarian usage. The pottery and porcelain, often salvaged by Rodia from rubbish dumps, is impressive in color and type. The artist loved bright and vivid color, and the tableware of that period, much of it produced in the USA, yielded maroon, blues and greens from the Mettox Company, pale colors and white from the local Los Angeles company of Bauer and Co., and orange, yellow and turquoise from the Harlequin and Fiesta companies, still in business today. There is also porcelain and china from the Far East, Japan and China, from where a beautiful hand-painted white plate, featuring a blue design with boats and pagoda, was embedded uncut into a structural soffit.

---

## Method

## Materials

a miscellany of glass, mirror glass,
 china, porcelain, tile and luster ware
 in a palette of gold and green
one single Roman tessera
epoxy resin – a two-component adhesive

spatula
dental prodder
protective gloves
narrow palette knives
mixing board

mosaic nippers
steel rule
glass cutter
glass pliers

1 All the material will be cut into tiny tesserae "gems". These will then be embedded into the pressed indents which have been made on the external horizontal and vertical bands and supports of the spire. Much of the material, i.e., the china, tile and porcelain, is cut in the usual way using the hand-held mosaic nippers.

**Secret Insight 3**

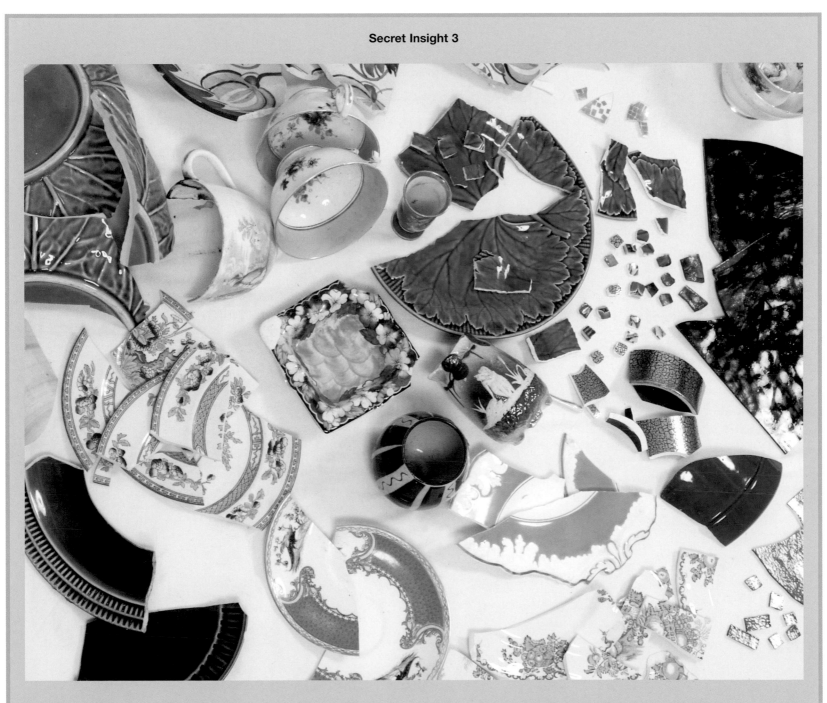

As an homage, I too have salvaged an exotic array of china and porcelain for inclusion in this work. Charity shops and local auction houses can yield to the mosaic artist a wondrous array of bounty. Included are chipped and broken gems from the great pottery companies of England, e.g., Maling, Newcastle on Tyne (1762-1963); British Anchor, England (1864-c.1960); Wedgwood, Stoke-on-Trent (1759 to the present); Sampson Smith, Longton, Staffordshire (1846-1963); Paragon Company in Stoke-on-Trent (1897 to the present); Paragon Rockingham, Stoke-on-Trent (mid to late 20th century); Myotts, Stoke-on-Trent (1898-1991); and replica china from the Victoria and Albert Museum shop in London.

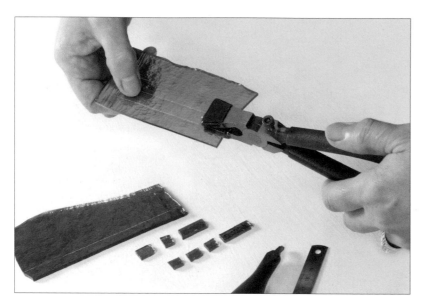

2 For the mirror glass use a glass cutter to score straight lines onto the sheets of mirror glass, and apply pressure with the glass pliers to fracture the glass cleanly in narrow bands before cutting these into small tesserae.

A spire is an arresting shape in itself, and has long been a symbol of aspiration, inspiration and divination for a wide variety of cultures and architects and artists.

Because of its very singular form, I felt the very complex construction of this particular spire with its internal tangle of metal required a very simple embellishment – as always in mosaic, simplicity is strength.

3 Using a two-component epoxy resin to bond the tesserae to the metal frame. The tiny tesserae or *tesserulae* were first fixed to the structure in shades of green mirror glass only, on the three horizontal bands. The two-component epoxy resin was mixed in small quantities at a time. A dental prodder was used to place each tessera in position.

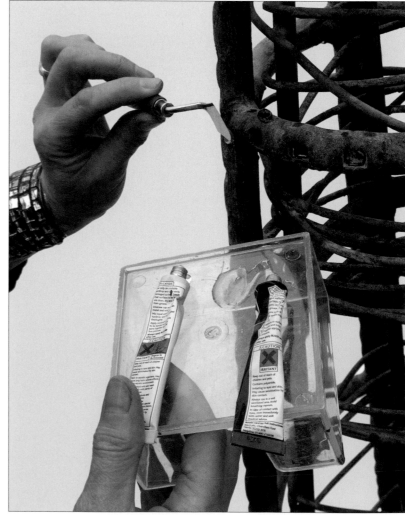

4 Aspects of the spire from four different angles. Each of the four outer upright supports was given a green and gold palette of about five different materials, repeated in a random design. Each tesserula was pressed into position using a small quantity of epoxy adhesive to secure the placing.

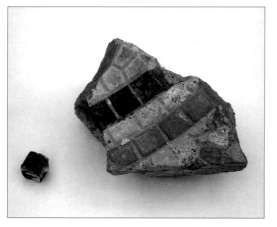

A fragment of a Roman mosaic with the single tessera used in the work.

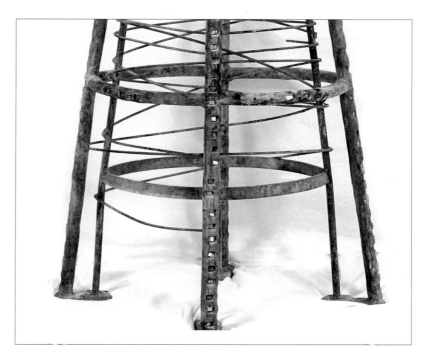

Detail: base

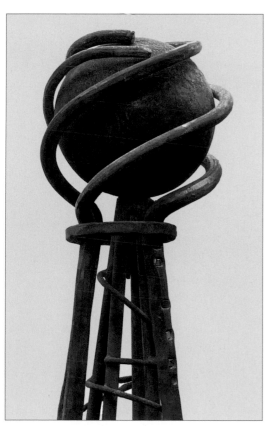

Detail: top

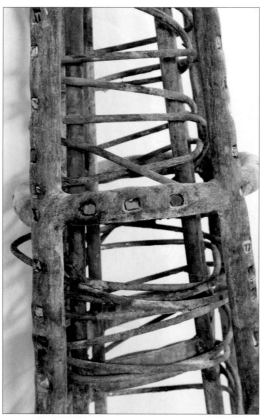

Detail: horizontal band

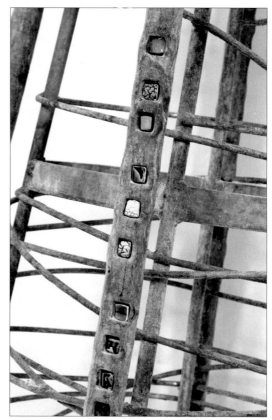

Detail: vertical support

# Personal & Self-Expression

## Historical Viewpoints

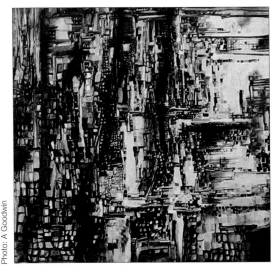

Photo: A Goodwin

Cité Ouvrière, *1956 by  Maria Elena Vieira da Silva*

By dematerializing a surface and breaking it up into a myriad facets of color and light, the enlightened Byzantine mosaic artists were to fling open a realm of understanding into the abstract qualities of visual art, long, long before its understanding among the artists of the 20th century.

Since this time, whether knowingly or not, artists of today have used the medium of mosaic to deepen their artistic understanding.  A number of painters have flirted with a mosaic-inspired approach in their work.  During the 1960s the English artist Wilhelmina Barns-Graham (1912-2004) cut squares of card, closely sequenced and spaced, to observe the interactions of form and hue, which she later transcribed to paintings of

superb intensity of rhythms and effect.

The Portuguese-born artist Maria Elena Vieira da Silva (1908-1992) was also adding mosaic-like squares of paint onto her canvases, creating intensely textural works in ethereal mono-tones of gray and silver.

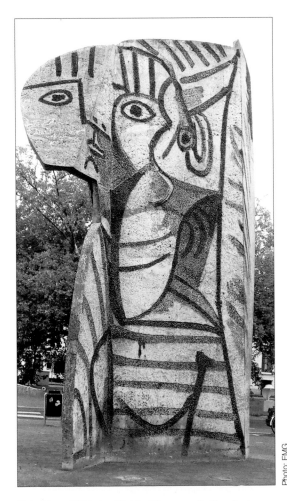

Photo: EMG

Sylvette, *1969, by Pablo Picasso, Rotterdam, Netherlands, beton (concrete), realized by Carl Nesjar (b. 1920)*

Perhaps best known is Pablo Picasso (1881-1973), but few know of his interest in mosaic. Late in the 1950s he began to sketch designs specifically for the medium, which were ably carried out in smalti and stone by Hjalmar Boyesen in his studio in Cannes.  Picasso, of course, understood that the strength of mosaic lies in simplicity.

One of his mosaic-like works can be seen today as a free-standing sculpture in Rotterdam in the Netherlands.

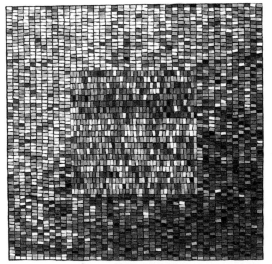

Photo: EMG

Pink, Green, Gold, *2007, by Giulio Candussio, Angelo Orsoni mosaic foundry, Venice, Italy*

Later in the 20th century other artists who, like Picasso, designed for mosaics but never personally worked on them in the making process were the Scottish/Italian sculptor Eduardo Paolozzi (1924-2005), and the English painter Howard Hodgkin (b. 1932).

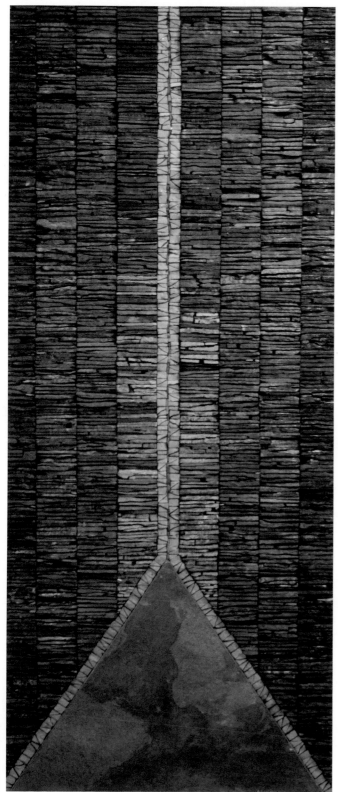

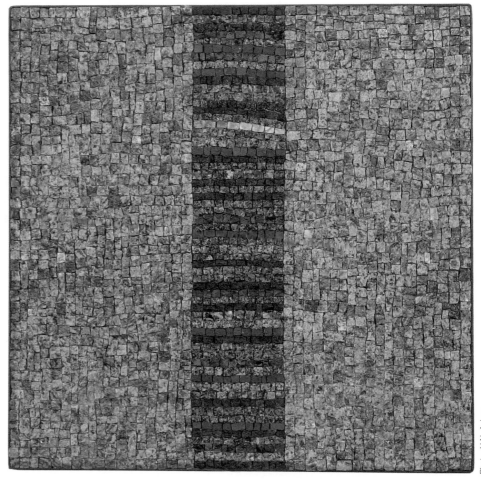

*Above:* Funambule III *by Henry-Noël Aubry, 2006, 19½in x 19½in/50cm x 50cm, marble and granite*

*Left:* Bifurcation *by Dugald MacInnes, 2007, 24in x 48in/60cm x 122cm, Scottish slate and Venetian smalti*

Paolozzi's designs for the Tottenham Court Road Underground station in 1983 were executed by a number of mosaic workshops and also by the master mosaicist Giulio Candusio (b. 1945), whose own personal work exudes light and scintillating surface movement.

Hodgkin's mural for the British Council headquarters in New Delhi, India, was created in close partnership with the Indian architect of the building, Charles Correa. It is made of hand cut tiles of marble and stone, and is a truly impressive covering for the façade of the building.

Of the work, Hodgkin wrote that his wish "was to make a design which would change dramatically when seen from different points of view."

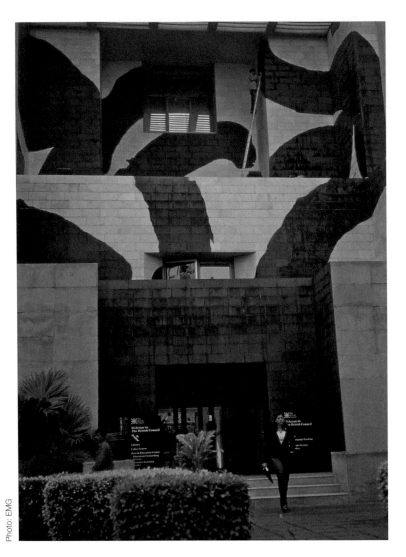

*Façade mural by
Sir Howard Hodgkin, 1992;
makrana marble, cudappah
stone, New Delhi, India*

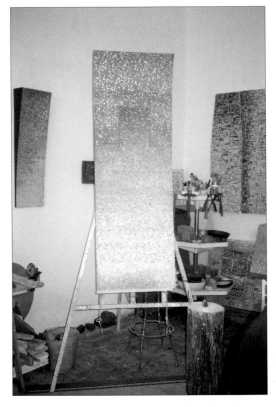

*Studio of Marco de Luca, 2007, Ravenna, Italy*

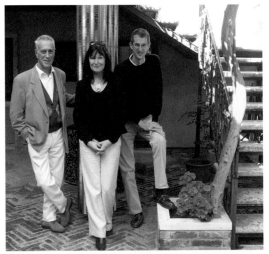

*Lucio Orsoni, the author, Luca Chiesura (administrator), at Angelo Orsoni, Venice, Italy, 2007, in front of a sculpture of smalti samples produced by the factory since 1888*

Yet it is only when mosaic is *released* from a wall and has the ability to be sited at will in any setting, that mosaic as an art form can really exist in its own right. Unlike paintings, tesserae panels can be positioned and placed to reflect light even in the dimmest of interiors, and this ability within the medium makes it transcend the pebble and stone tesserae of the floors and pavings of the Greeks and Romans, and introduces a most powerful responsibility for the medium – that of conjurer of light.

Outstanding exponents working today and taking singular directions for mosaic as personal expression are relatively few. Among them are Verdiano Marzi (b. 1949) and Henry-Noël Aubry (b. 1960) in Paris, France; Dugald MacInnes (b. 1952) in Stirling, Scotland; Marco de Luca in Ravenna, Italy (b. 1949) and Lucio Orsoni (b. 1939) in Venice, Italy.

Dugald MacInnes was a pupil of the pioneering Edinburgh-born mosaic artist George Garson (b. 1930) whose mural work can be seen at Glasgow School of Art and the University of Glasgow, Scotland. Dugald works exclusively in locally-sought slate from Argyllshire, which he combines with traditional Venetian glass smalti and gold leaf. His works have a timeless quality evoking profound certainties of being.

Henry-Noël Aubry, like Verdiano Marzi, trained in Paris in the studio of Riccardo Licata, a master mosaicist who himself was the pupil of Gino Severini (b. 1883), the Italian forerunner of a modern movement and expression for mosaic. Aubry's work is suffused in concepts of nature, revering its strength and pervasiveness, yet his materials of granite and marble emit a *sensitivo* and delicate beauty and order.

Ravenna-born, Marco de Luca is a poet of light. In his works each irregular tessera of marble, gold and shard of glass is tentatively laid, poised and balanced, like the words and rhythm of eternal poems.

The Venetian artist Lucio Orsoni creates works of outstanding vitality, which pulse with light and color. Devoid of sentiment they are constructed of the simplest hand cut unit, the square – the tessera – in the purest of *opus tessellatum*.

What of the future for this medium *par excellence*? It is for you, the artist and reader, to ensure for it a continuing eminent role in the visual arts.

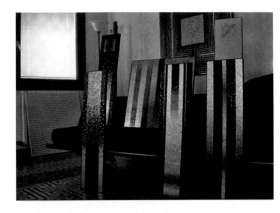

*Studio of Lucio Orsoni, 2007, Cannaregio, Venice, Italy*

# Inspirations from Contemporary Artists

The following highly acclaimed artists use the mosaic medium for their very personal voice, finding within the medium uniquely expressive ways to expound their visual concepts.

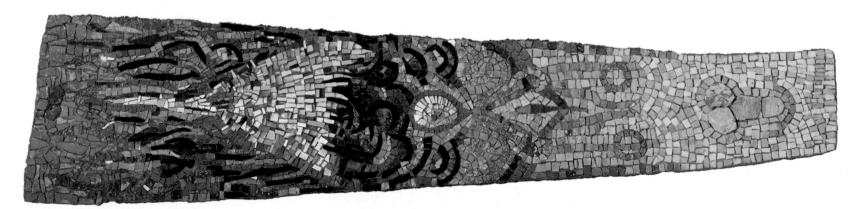

**Dilindara I - Magic Flower**, 2007,
10½in x 36in / 27cm x 91cm,
kilned glass, stones, ceramic

**Gazanfer Bayram**
Born in Skopje (former Republic of Yugoslavia), 1948. Lives and works in Skopje, Republic of Macedonia.

*Artist's Statement, Skopje, Macedonia, 2007*
Stone to stone... mosaic is a re-animation; it inspires the soul of the stone. Mosaic, like the phoenix, regenerates itself through history.

The play of light that radiates from the stone and its miraculous colors replaces my painter's palette. The contrasts of materials in contemporary mosaic are the embrace of man and nature.

My dance with the stone is unceasing.

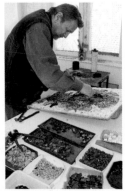

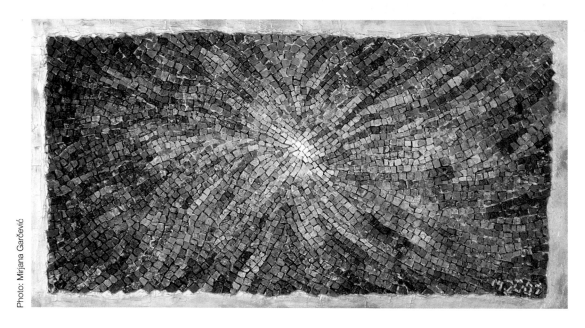

Photo: Mirjana Garčević

**Homage à Peter Fischer**, 2007, 14in x 27½in /35cm x 70cm, multi-colored marbles, stones and brick

### Milun Garčević
Born in Andrijevica, Croatia (former Yugoslavia), 1959. Lives and works in Zagreb, Croatia.

*Artist's Statement, Zagreb, Croatia, 2007*
The late Peter Fischer mentioned in one of his critiques that mosaic was the medium for the third millennium! That opinion I share, without any doubt. Mosaic today is without conventions and more able to be original. It is possible to experiment with new forms and new materials alongside traditional techniques. Mosaic is not just *pittura per l'éternita,* but *l'arte per l' éternita.*

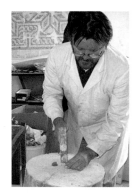

### Ilia Iliev
Born in Bourgas, Bulgaria, in 1931. Lives and works in Sofia, Bulgaria.

*Artist's Statement, Sofia, Bulgaria, 2007*
The fight between Geometry and Nature dominates my personal work. The geometry and logic stem from my time studying architecture, My love of nature and the sea is deeply entrenched in my heart. The contest between logic and feeling never stops – sometimes happy moments of harmony occur, for which the principal cause is the choice of materials used.

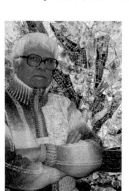

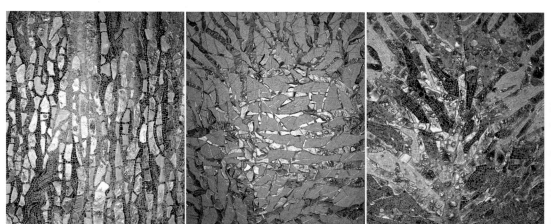

Photos: Maria Ilieva Boteva Deni Krastev

**Triptych** 2006-7, 177in x 110in/450cm x 280cm, kilned glass, stones, ceramic

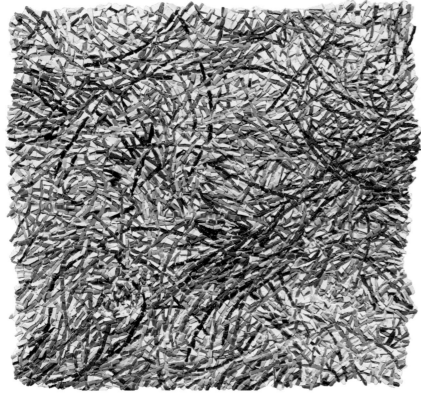

## Toyoharu Kii

Born in Ehime, Japan, in 1953. Lives and works in Tokyo, Japan.

*Artist's Statement, Tokyo, JapanI, 2007*
I want to express movement; air and light, in mosaic. In this new work, the light penetrates through the grass – and the atmosphere moves. Another theme must be the beauty of the smalti!

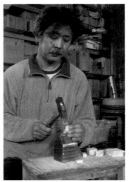

***The Wind Blows Grass***, 2007,
18in x 18in/45cm x 45cm; smalti, marble

Photos: Toyoharu Kii

## Edda Mally

Born in Austria, 1930s. Lives and works in Vienna, Austria

*Artist's Statement, Vienne, Austria, 2007*
Artworks, specially paintings and mosaics, are for me objects of high energetic power. Expressive forms and colors in many variations express fundamental ideas. Artistic work means the momentary capturing of an image or event that reveals my personal interpretation. I try to catch different effects of light and shadow, using the three dimensional and rough surfaces.

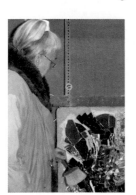

Photo: EMG

***Eye of Cosmos***,
37in x 29in x 8in /
95cm x 73cm x 20cm,
marble, glass, fabrics
and copper

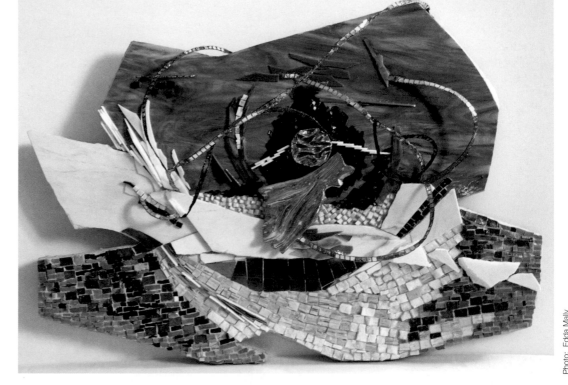

Photo: Edda Mally

# Bird Within/Without a Cage

## Inspiration

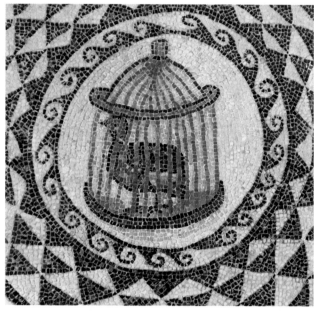

Photo: EMG

*Small caged bird (partridge), 4th-5th century AD, Bardo Museum, Tunis, Tunisia*

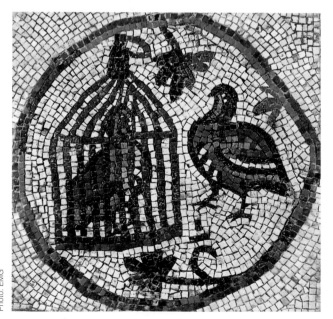

Photo: EMG

*Bird within a cage and bird without, 6th century AD. The lower mosaics of the North Church, Hesban (Esbus), Jordan*

## Background Revelations

The Romans loved to use bird imagery in their designs, sometimes drawing from reality or using the bird as a symbol.

This image of a captive small bird intrigues me… The representation of a bird in a cage, often with a second bird outside the cage looking in, appears in many Roman floors throughout the Mediterranean. The bird motif is most often identified as a partridge. It is possible that the image was merely a simple hunting one, used metaphorically as a lure – but it can have deeper symbolic meanings, one of which the Romans were well aware – depending on where the image occurs. If sited in a *cubiculum* (bedroom), the Aphrodisian symbolism becomes apparent. The erotic capacities of a partridge were well known…. As a metaphysical evocation of freedom, too, it had me thinking.

The tradition of having a caged bird in the home is a popular one, even today. In living rooms, courtyards and balconies throughout Europe and North Africa the sound of a cooing lovebird or the song of a canary can add a welcome note.

As a simple image to live with, knowing of these deeper meanings is for me the continuation of the appeal of this motif. Where the cage is composed of mirror, this begins an enquiry, adding ambiguous and uncertain visual aspects.

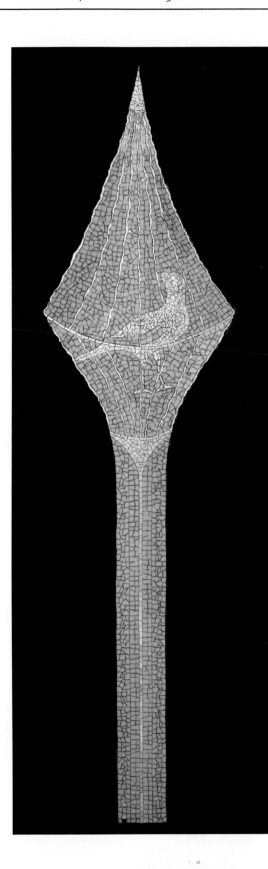

The Completed Work

From time to time the light catches the circular silver tesserae of the "song". A simple *trompe l'oeil* effect is created. Depending on the play of light, too, the bars of the cage both hold the bird captive and at other times release it, even its song.

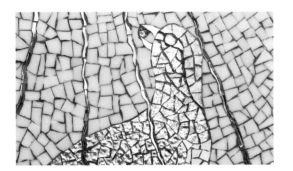

A Favorite poem of mine is by the French poet Jacques Prévert (1900-1977):

### To Paint the Portrait of a Bird

First paint a cage
with an open door
then paint
something pretty
something simple
something beautiful
something useful…
for the bird
then place the canvas against a tree
in a garden
in a wood
or in a forest
hide behind the tree
without speaking
without moving…
Sometimes the bird comes quickly
but he can just as well spend long years
before deciding
Don't get discouraged
wait
wait years if necessary
the swiftness or slowness of the coming
of the bird having no rapport
with the success of the picture
When the bird comes
if he comes

observe the most profound silence
wait till the bird enters the cage
and when he has entered
gently close the door with a brush
then
paint out all the bars one by one
taking care not to touch any of the feathers of
the bird
Then paint the portrait of the tree
choosing the most beautiful of its branches
for the bird
paint also the green foliage and the wind's
freshness
the dust of the sun
and the noise of insects in the summer heat
and then wait for the bird to decide to sing
If the bird doesn't sing
it's a bad sign
a sign that the painting is bad
but if he sings it's a good sign
a sign that you can sign
so then so very gently you pull out
one of the feathers of the bird
and you write your name in a corner of the
picture.

## Method

### The Drawing

1 The bars of the "cage" were drawn – but as broken lines. These will be constructed of glass mirror, adding an element of speculation and of enquiry; metaphysical elements of liberty and captivity; what is here or not here, and so on.

The drawing is made on a shaped piece of plywood forming a "cage" and stand.

Draw a bird – any bird – as a symbol of "birdness", a being of flight, and therefore permanence/impermanence. Also add a "song", by drawing small circles as rising notes.

Firm up the drawing with a felt-tipped marker pen.

### Equipment

long T-square ruler
pencil
eraser
permanent marker

### Materials

½in/12mm exterior plywood cut to shape
  64in/163cm  x 16in/40cm
mirror tiles
Venetian white gold-leaf (silver) – plain,
  ribbed, granulated and wavy
silver mirrors with a variety of finishes or
  silver-glazed tiles

white vitreous glass mosaic
wheeled mosaic nippers
pva adhesive/white glue
palette knife
container

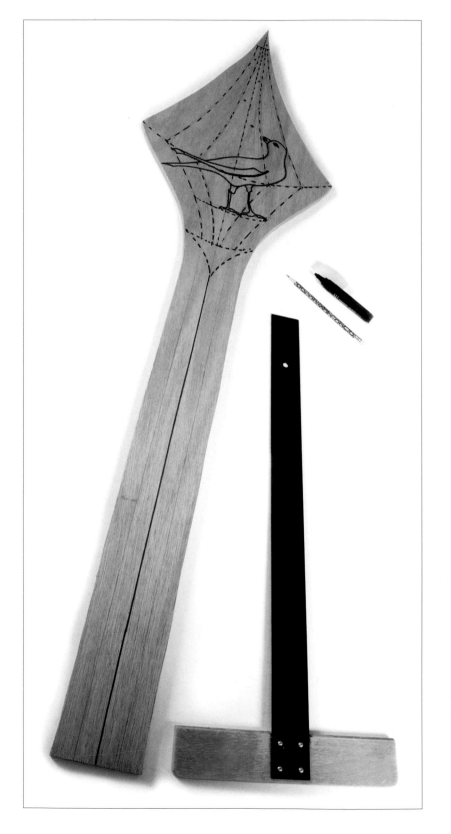

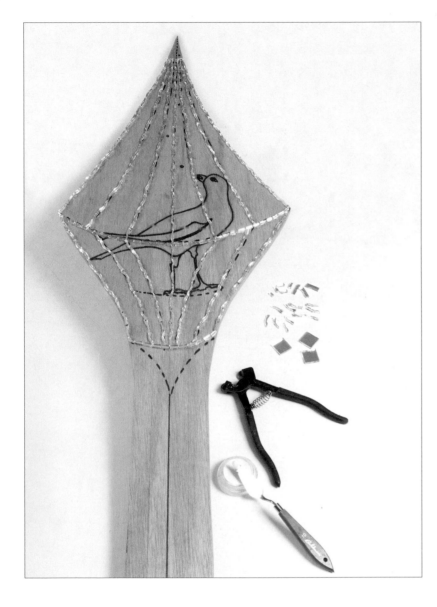

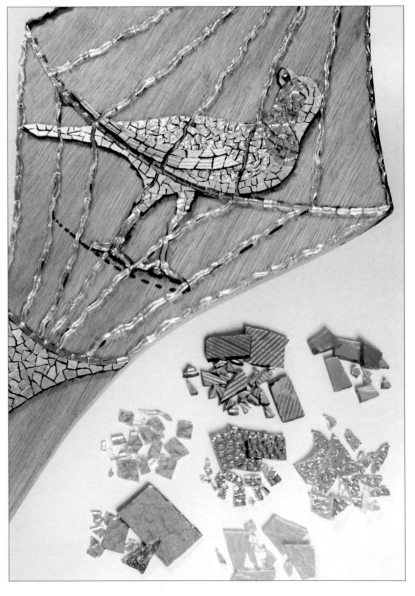

2 The mirror tiles were cut both as undulating ribbons and as small rectangular strips. Use the cut mirror ribbons to make up the vertical bars of the cage – the irregular outline will help in giving a sense of ambiguity as to their presence. Use the straight edged small rectangular tesserae, however, to form the horizontal bars to give some hint of structure to the cage area. The tip and "stand" of the cage are also completed with silver-glazed tesserae.

3 The bird was created using a widely textured palette of silver-leaf gold and mirror with varying surface finishes. Its "song" was made using four cut circles of mirror glass.

The patina of silver which makes up the body of the bird again inclines towards ambiguity – in some lights the bird appears to be almost invisible, and at other times, at night or in low light, overly pronounced. This sense of instability so latent within the reflecting materials of gold and mirror begin a metaphysical enquiry even though the image is a natural one – one drawn from nature and not abstract in itself.

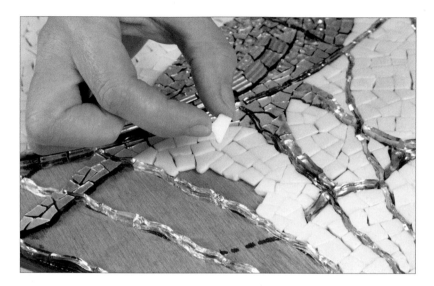

4 A simple white vitreous glass was used for all the background. The mosaic is to be positioned on a white painted wall, so again the choice of white was very deliberate for at times both the wall and the background will merge, giving very little indication as to the existence of the latter. *Opus palladianum* was used, as the randomly-cut shapes cope well with the variously shaped areas to be covered.

5 A single tessera cut loosely into four was the unit used to form an initial band of mosaic on either side of the silver line indicating the stand. The remaining area was again finished in *opus palladianum*, placing the edges with straight sides first at the outside edge, before filling in the remaining area.

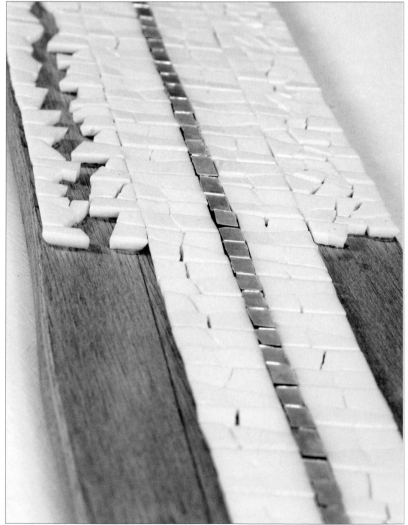

# Grouting

## Materials

a proprietary cement grout    protective gloves

container    water

trowel    silicon buffing cloth

cloths

6  Make up a quantity of cement mortar, adding water slowly to the cement grout, forming a 'not too wet' mix. Wearing protective gloves, rub this into all the interstices, taking special care around the bird. Clean and leave to cure under damp cloths before a final clean with water, 2-3 days later.

    Buff the surface with the silicon cloth to clear any residue cement scum from the surface of the materials, and bring maximum gloss to the mirror, glass and silver.

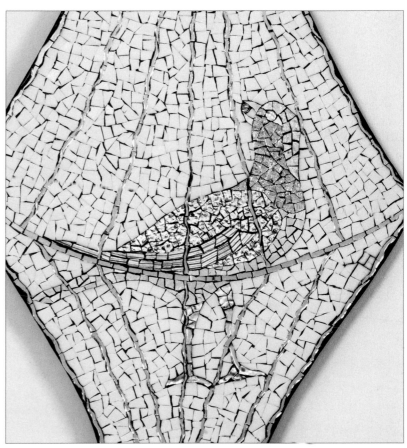

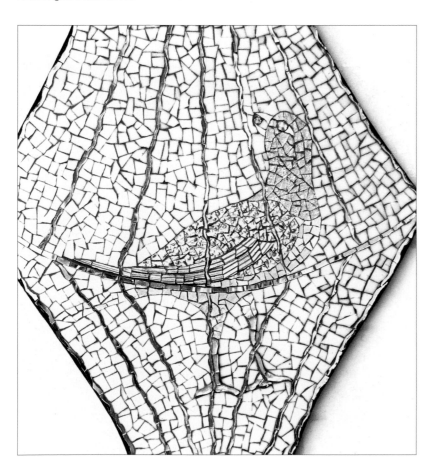

I was anxious to compare the mosaic in both its ungrouted state (above) and grouted state (left), and to note the subtle yet discernable difference. It is important at all times to experiment, and to keep experimenting and recording for future reference. Learning the art of mosaic should be a continually living process – never a question of unconsidered copying or imitative facsimile making. It should be experienced and explored and enjoyed.

# Particles

## The Inspirational Mosaic

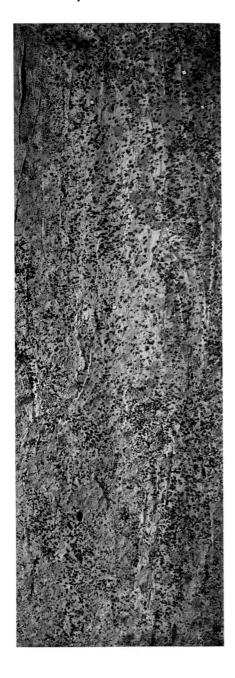

*Left:* Remission *by Jeanne Reynal, 1962, 78in x 27in / 198cm x 69cm, smalti, marble tesserae, private collection, USA*

## Background Revelations

For me, the New York artist Jeanne Reynal (1903-1983) is the first true modern artist in mosaic. She supports much of what I believe is possible for the medium – yet in her own very personal direction, evoking also the era in which she lived. She takes the art of mosaic making to an extreme which is, however, based soundly on the integrity of the medium. Her personal investigation into mosaic making in both her 3D and 2D work, led her deeper and deeper into its latent potential, as a supreme medium for self-expression.

Jeanne Reynal began her practical learning of the medium of mosaic under the instruction of Boris Anrep (1885-1969), the great Russian émigré, a maestro of the indirect method of mosaic application. She had previously traveled extensively in Europe, studying by looking, the mosaics of Sicily, Italy and France.

For eight years (1950-1958) she learned about techniques at Anrep's Paris studio where she met artists like Pablo Picasso (1881-1973), Joan Miró (1893-1983), and Fernand Léger (1881-1955). The indirect method used extensively in Anrep's studio, which she eagerly mastered, depended for its effect on color, design and *andamento* within a flat surface – but by the 1960s (having worked independently as a mosaic artist back in the United States), she was saying,

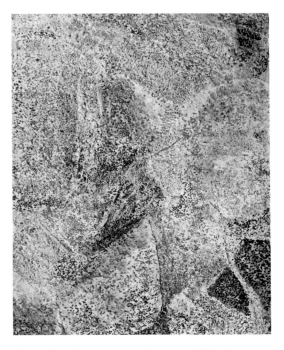

Pastel Sonata *by Jeanne Reynal, 1956-57, 60in x 48in /153cm x 122cm, smalti, marble, Syracuse University collection*

"Contrary to opinions previously held by me, I hope to show that the medium of mosaic is not painting with stones and not sculpture but an art the essential quality of which is luminosity." What had happened?

Today, as then, many artists have tried to reproduce only the techniques of historical mosaic work, ignoring the aesthetic needs of their own time. Jeanne Reynal however, was determined to release the medium from its additive process and to find in it a contemporary voice – as her artist friends, Mark Rothko (1903-1970), Arshile Gorky (1904-1948), and Willem de

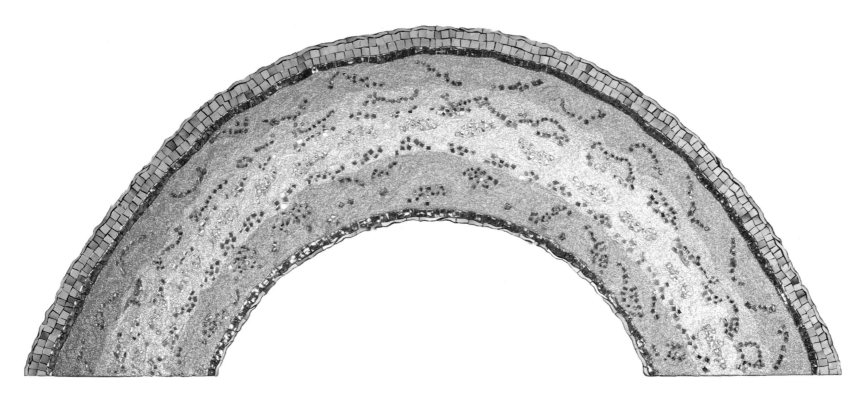

The Completed Work – *Particles.*
In this work, as in that of the artist Jeanne Reynal, the work addresses us diversely – perhaps through the intellect, the senses, or the emotions.   The work is to be looked "at" and "into".   There are only hints to assist the "looking" – perhaps the title of the piece, or perhaps the form. The best appreciation depends on unity with an open and perceptive mind.

Jeanne Reynal pushed mosaic as far as it could go in one direction, liberating the traditionally controlled media of mosaic and setting free the tesserae to exist by chance, randomly, on a cement bed.  The golden arc of light particles pays part homage to her extreme technique, but retains elements of historical restraint.  It is up to each of us to find a personal bag of gold at the end of the rainbow of light and color she created.

Kooning (1904-1997) were doing with painting. She wanted to push the boundaries far from what she felt were the academic limitations of the medium.

Jeanne Reynal was for ever experimenting: from working with transparent plastic, which allowed the tesserae to be fixed as free-form sculpture on two surfaces, to what she is most remembered for – free action mosaics.  In these she freely drops fragments of smalti and Venetian gold or marble onto a mortar,  a white Portland cement pre-colored with pigment, to create surfaces of intricate and living texture and light.  Her friend the artist Jackson Pollock (1912-1956) was

dribbling paint onto large canvases in much the same manner.  But she worked with a difference: while some tesserae were left flat, others she angled into a cement mortar by lightly tapping them in or pressing them deep into the backing mortar, using a rubber hammer.  With these works she felt she had achieved her aim – to create surfaces of living light which 'breathed' with a unique spatial quality – an achievement exclusively reserved for the mosaic medium.

*Reincarnation Lullaby, 1961, by Jeanne Reynal, 53in  x 53in /135cm x 135cm, private collection, New York, USA*

## Method

### The Drawing

Because I associate Jeanne Reynal with color and light, I wished for the form to be arc-shaped, to evoke a rainbow and its attending attributes of ever-moving color and light.

My own sensibilities do not permit me to 'dribble' the tesserae into a mastic – too much of a liberation? – but I shall endeavor to create an arc of light in my own defining material – gold – coloring the mortar as she did and working at times with a loose tessellation.

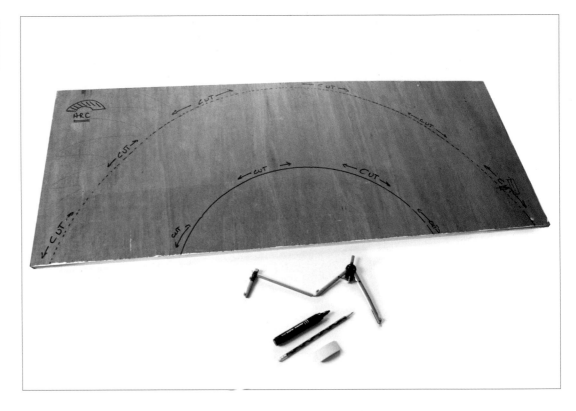

1 Use the compasses to draw two arcs on the timber, forming an arched shape.  Firm up the edges to be cut using a permanent marker pen.

### Equipment

large format compass
pencil
marker pen
eraser
electric hand-held jigsaw
glass paper/sandpaper

### Materials

½in/12mm exterior plywood
Gold ink
brush
container
gold glass/iridescent stained glass and
   gold mirror glass
standard silvered glass mirror
wheeled nippers

white Portland cement
various golds and silver glitter
a selection of palette knives
pva adhesive/white glue
black sealer
dental prodder
proprietary sealer

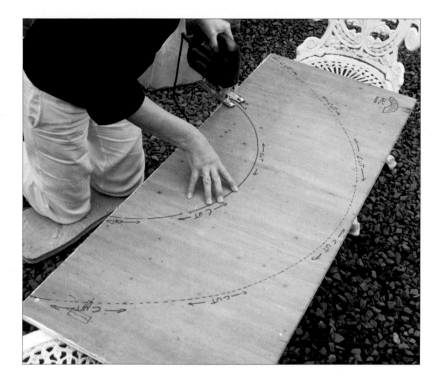

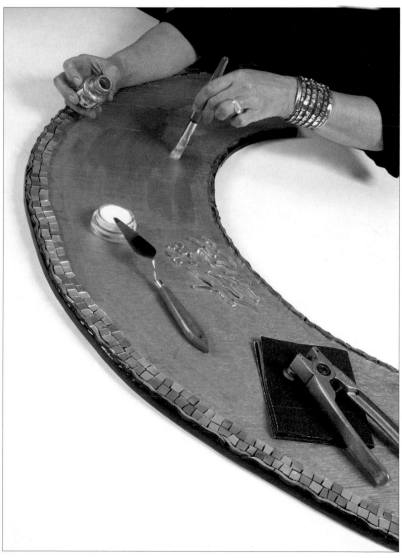

2 Begin to cut out the shape using a hand-held electric jig-saw. The shape is carefully cut, tracing the saw blade along the marker lines. Keep a steady continuous motion when cutting a curved shape to give the smoothest possible result. These cut edges may need to be sanded down before being worked on.

3 Painting the timber with gold ink. Cut the gold glass or stained glass to form both undulating ribbons and squares of tesserae. Use the former to outline the arc's upper and lower edges, before lining the upper arc with a line of tesserae in the same material. I felt the shape needed some sort of defining border frame, even one with an uneven edge, inside which a mortar with a fairly random design could be created – an idea at this stage very hard for me to relish!

A further line of mirror glass in a rich gold was added at both the top and bottom of the arc, a device I'm sure was included by me to stave off the moment before the random act of 'dribbling' or dropping the tesserae began.

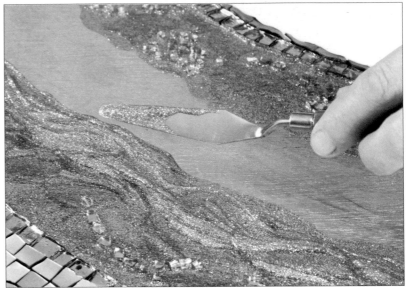

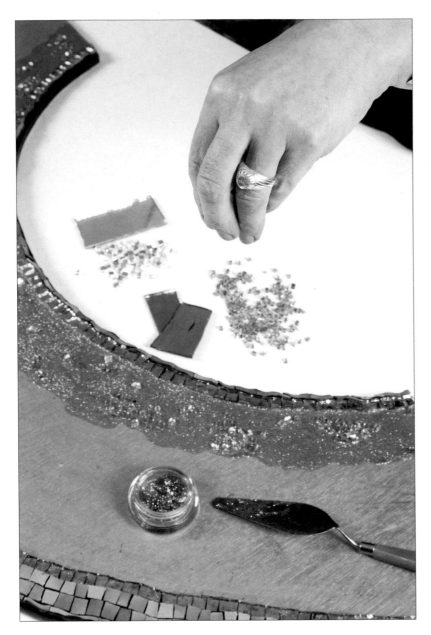

4 Dropping the tiny mirror glass tesserae at intervals into the setting bed. The setting bed that receives the fragments of "dribbled" tesserae will be colored, as in the Reynal mosaics. A small quantity of white Portland cement, golden glitter and white glue/pva was mixed together. The cement was added cautiously as I did not want the glitter to lose optimal color effect. Experiment with the ratio of each to each and note the result, for possible later applications in your work.

5 Continue to add lines of glittery background mortar, sometimes of a different hue, using a narrow-headed palette knife. The palette knife is a wonderful little tool. The flexible metal head can be pointed, rounded, narrow, squat, elongated, slanted – each designed for an impressive number of uses. Collect a variety, and again, experiment with each to learn the scope and limitations of each shape – soon the little gadget will be like a flexible friend – a dexterous extension of your drawing hand.

The central part of the arc has a silvery setting bed. Into this adhesive "dribble" tesserae shards of silver-backed glass or mirror – some tesserae a little larger than the rest. Stand back from the work – or lay it on the floor to get an overall effect.

When using this 'dribbling' technique on a larger work, lay it on the ground, allowing for good access on all sides. A wonderful sense of freedom and rhythm can be experienced when bending over the work and letting go the loosely-held tesserae. How you "dribble" can be as controlled or uncontrolled as you wish. The work is 'finished' only when you, the creator, knows it is. This will be an instinctive visual judgment which you must allow to happen. Again, do not be deterred – the work will dictate its own end.

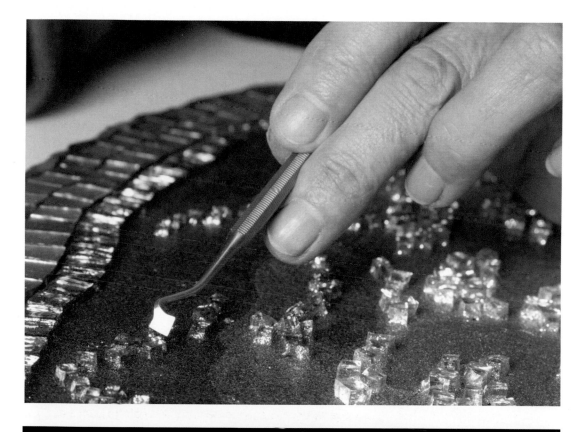

6 When regarding the finished work, you may feel it necessary to very gently tap or press single tesserae in an inward, outward, upward or downward direction to catch or deflect the light. I find a flat angle-ended dental prodder invaluable.

When dry, seal all the edges of the wood with a proprietary sealer. There will be no frame as such, as this would curtail the elusive quality inherent in the image.

## Concerning Experimentation

Do not at any time be afraid to experiment with materials and adhesives, pigments and cements – in this way you will feel more intimately connected with what you are doing and will build up a personal reserve of techniques and adhesives which you can use to uniquely characterize your work. Be assured, not all experimentation yields positive results, as I can well testify – but don't be deterred.

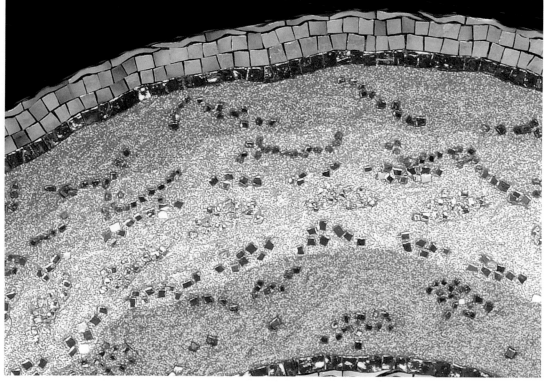

Detail from the finished work

# Light Modules

## Inspiration

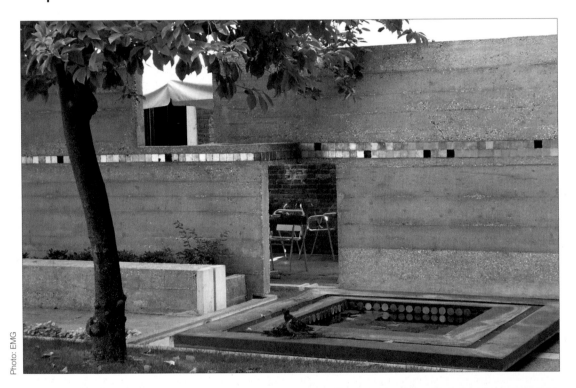

*Palazzo Querini Stampalia, 1961-63, by Carlo Scarpa, garden wall detail showing the mosaic detailing, Venice, Italy*

Photo: EMG

> ### Secret Insight I
>
> Scarpa had an obsession with the 2¼in/5.5cm module and its multiples, so much so that it became in effect his signature. He used it as a continual point of reference (that it deviated from the accepted norm of 2in/5cm amused him). When using mosaic of Venetian metallic gold in his work, he often doubled up the uncut square plates to emphasize this modular unit – two squares are approximately 6½in/16.5cm, an exact tripling of his 5.5 unit of measurement.

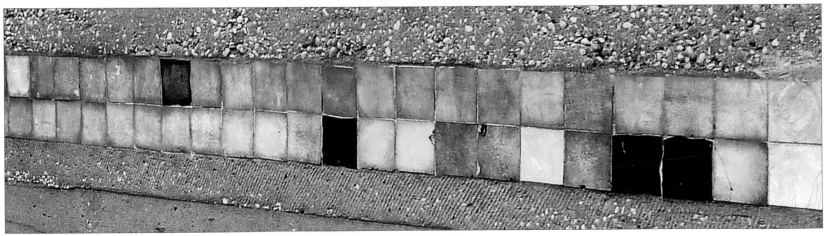

*A double band of uncut Venetian metallic gold and silver, detail, Querini Stampalia Foundation, Venice, Italy*

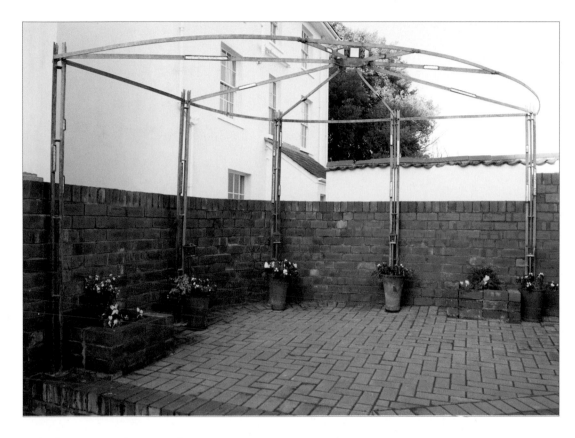

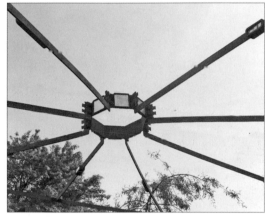

The Completed Work – *Light Modules*
The structure of the pergola is articulated with playful rhythms of light modules which give definition to its structure, both vertically and in space. A vine will be trained to cover the pergola, through which, in time, the notes of silvery visual music can be enjoyed.

# Background Revelations

The Venetian architect Carlo Scarpa (1906-1979) celebrated life! He had the ability to articulate a space with carefully chosen materials which expressed delight through color, texture, pattern, and above all light – elements dear to the heart of a mosaic artist. He created vital relationships of assonance and dissonance, forming visual volumetric and surface rhythms, for example, light-dark, rough-smooth, glass-concrete, color-monotone. But above all he was

### Secret Insight 2

You may notice the dark squares in the otherwise gold and silver linear design of the Querini Stampalia detailing. These are not an introduced color… they are proof that mosaic is not always made of infallible materials, but of sensitive handmade materials like Venetian gold leaf glass. As in Byzantine churches, where similar patches occur among the golden expanses, it means that the surface glass – the *cartellina* – protecting the precious gold leaf underneath, has come away. The gold leaf has rubbed off or weathered away, exposing the colored backing glass – in this case of a deep black color.

aware that it was articulated light which gave life to his work – and for this I salute him.

Carlo Scarpa's work emits playful eloquence. There is an intrinsic vitality which enlivens the formal and geometric elegance of his designs. He was a great admirer of the architect Josef Hoffman, architect of the Palais Stoclet in Brussels, and he investigated thoroughly his masterly handling of forms. He absorbed, too, the refined sensibilities of Japanese architecture, in particular the Imperial Palace of Katsura in Kyoto, Japan, with its seeming simplicity and where all the spatial elements appear harmonious.

Scarpa was naturally familiar with mosaic work, particularly the materials of Venetian gold and glass smalti – so expansively used in St Mark's Cathedral in the Campo San Marco of Venice. For him, mosaic gave profile to edges, defining walls with specific proportions of height as well as giving light or color to surrounding concrete or stone surfaces.

In the Palazzo Querini Stampalia light plays a seminal role. This is particularly noticeable both on the ground floor and in the garden, where light reverberates off the canal at the front and the garden pool at the back. His use of metallic gold and silver, which edges the pool and defines the portico wall, is not only formally restrained but dazzlingly exuberant.

## Concerning the Form

The form was made to fit a pre-defined external south-facing sitting area. An iron pergola was thought to give shape, height and enclosure to the space, which would be enlivened with inserts of Venetian metallic glass, thus playing with the elements of brick (wall), iron (pergola), and metallic gold (defining features).

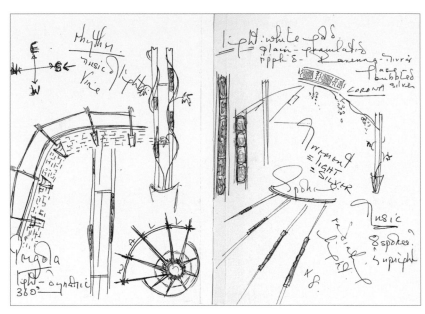

The author's sketchbook pages (right) give some insights into the development of the idea.

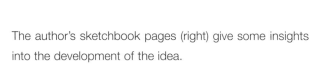

# Method

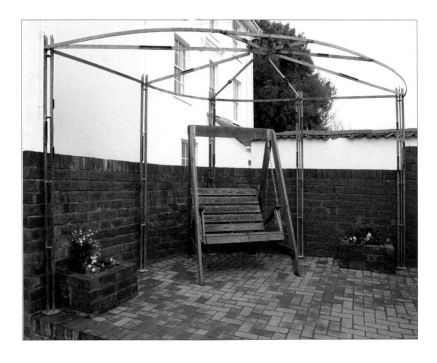

## The Design

1 The area after construction with the pergola and its metallic inserts. The metal sculptor, Richard Bent, has created a pergola to be as open as possible at the front, exposing five metal uprights holding narrow metallic inserts. Like five musical staves, these rectangular inserts are set at varying intervals like notes – I propose to translate them into "light notes", embedding highly reflective metallic and mirror mosaic, articulating light as musical intervals. The metal roofing bands of the pergola also contain metallic inserts and will continue the theme of light reflective mosaic "notes", with the ability to be seen from all angles as radiated and rhythmic music.

At the apex of the pergola, an eight-sided corona stabilizes the design and crowns it. Here, eight culminating square metallic inserts create the possibility for light to be reflected outward, like a beacon in a circle of light. By articulating light in mosaic making in this way, the formalized notions that Carlo Scarpa used in his work can be sustained, developed and celebrated.

## Materials

| | |
|---|---|
| manufactured unglazed ceramic | wheeled nippers |
|    tesserae ¾in/18mm | clean plastic sheeting |
| Ravenna mirror glass | paper |
| Venetian white gold, plain and rippled | rulers |
| antique Venetian white gold | marker pen |
| epoxy resin | pencils |
| pva/white glue | fiber netting |
| containers | scissors |
| spatulas | brush |
| standard nippers | buffing cloth |

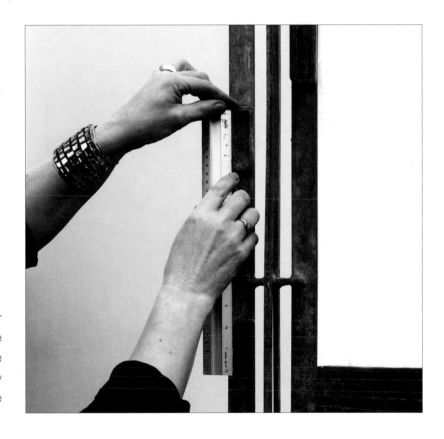

2 Measuring the metal inserts for template-making. The rectangular metal inserts were deeply embedded in the structure, allowing a base template to be made for each on which the mosaic could be made. There were five varying lengths, so five paper templates were made for each by measuring the length and width of the inserts, and cutting the shape accordingly, from a sheet of white paper.

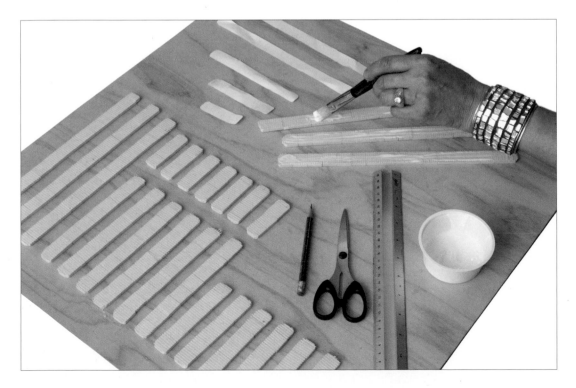

3 The width of each insert was the width of a manufactured unglazed ceramic tessera, which greatly facilitated the making of the templates. These were simply made by putting clear plastic and fiber netting over the paper template, and constructed accordingly. There were 33 templates in total. When dry each was turned over and the plastic peeled off. The back of each template was then brushed quite thickly with pva/white glue which, when dry, would form a rigid and continuous backing.

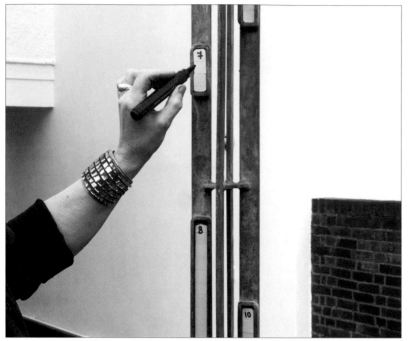

4 Each template was individually carried to site, placed in position, checked for size, and then numbered sequentially with the marker pen. This was necessary as each metallic insert had slight nuances of size difference. A note was taken of any variation in length where this occurred, and accommodated at the time of making.

5 The panel of completed modules alongside examples of the materials from which they were made. The facing side of each template was worked on in mosaic materials of a highly reflective nature, either white gold or mirror glass, using pva / white glue to adhere each in position. Each of the five lengths, or modules, was given a different material as each corresponded to a varying "note" of light.

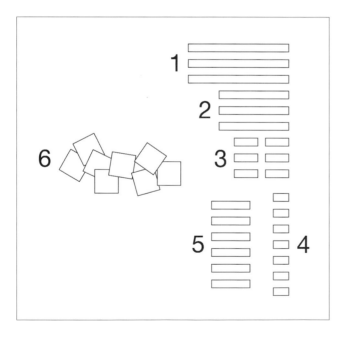

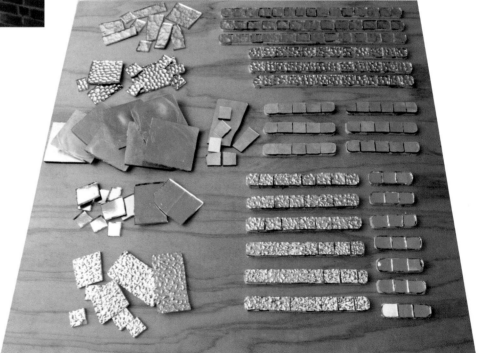

Key to the materials used for the light modules

1. Ravenna mirror glass – plain
2. Ravenna mirror glass – patterned
3. Venetian white gold leaf – plain
4. Ravenna mirror glass – clear
5. Venetian white gold leaf – granulated
6. Antique Venetian white gold leaf

6 The finished modules were fixed in position using a two-component epoxy resin, allowing the base ceramic template to adhere well to the metal of the pergola.  Gradually, as each "note" was placed both on the uprights and in the roofing inserts, the modules of light began to "sing out" in their constructed rhythm.

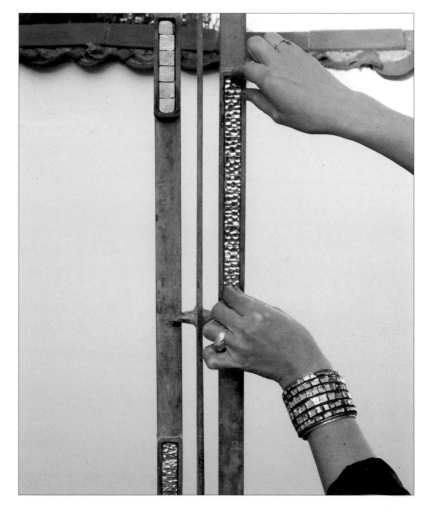

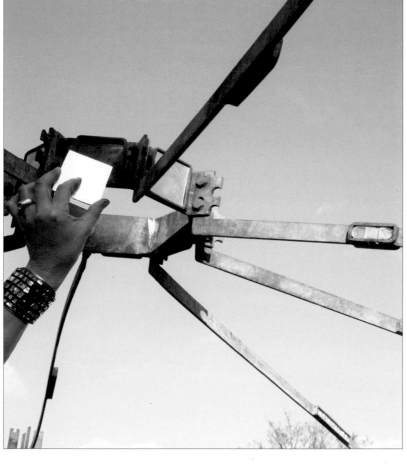

7 The corona, or metal crown was composed of eight square inserts of approximately 2¾in/7cm.  Eight pieces of plain antique Venetian white gold were cut to size for this – an appropriately luscious material for the culminating apex of the design.

# Windows of Perception

## The Inspirational Mosaic

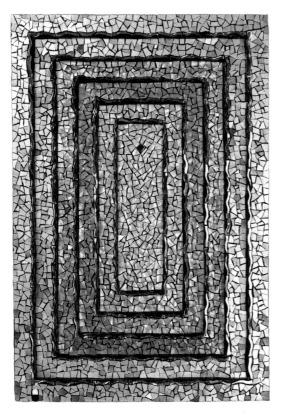

Fenêtre sur la Perception I
*(Window of Perception I), 2006,
by Elaine M Goodwin,
18in x 12in/46cm x 30cm*

*The secular panel of the Emperor Justinian and
his courtiers, San Vitale, Ravenna, Italy,
6th century AD*

## Background Revelations

Artists have from time immemorial worked on particular themes and recurring images throughout their creative lives. These are concepts and motifs which impress themselves on the mind impermeably. One such subject of thought for me is the window – but the window without matter, purely as a concept, a challenge which I feel mosaic can rise to.

There have been two turning points in my developing life as an artist. The first owes its allegiance to the Roman art of mosaic, which initiated my interest in the medium, and the second to the Byzantine art of mosaic which remains with me today.

This second turning point occurred in the mid-1980s, when I was in Ravenna looking at the early Byzantine mosaics of Galla Placidia and specifically San Vitale. These sixth-century mosaics of richly colored glass smalti and glowing metallic gold were awe-inspiring.

Then suddenly something extraordinary happened – as I looked I had a conviction that I knew the secret of life! I began to laugh and ran outside. An old man came up to me and touched my arm, asking, *"Che cosa c'e?"* (What's the matter?) I explained I was an artist and had suddenly realized the meaning of life from looking at the mosaics and seeing – only light! He answered *"Ma naturalmente"* (But of course). This man was none other than the esteemed mosaic master,

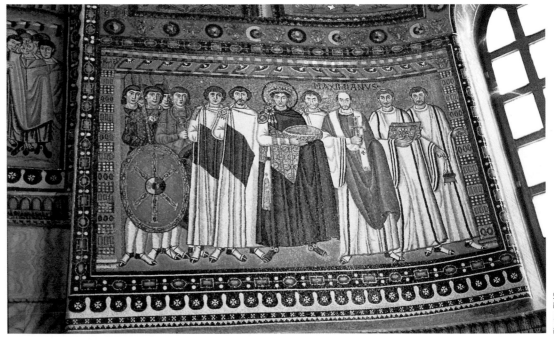

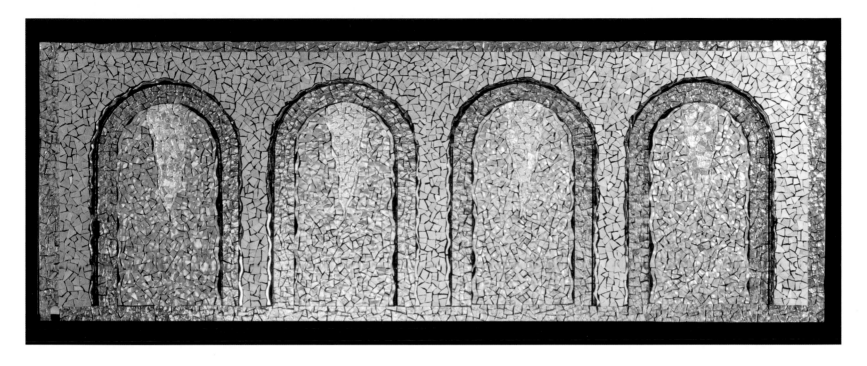

The Completed Work

*Intimations of Light I*, 2007. A new addition to my pantheon of "windows" for reflection and contemplation.

And, below, is shown another: *Intimations of Light II*, 2007

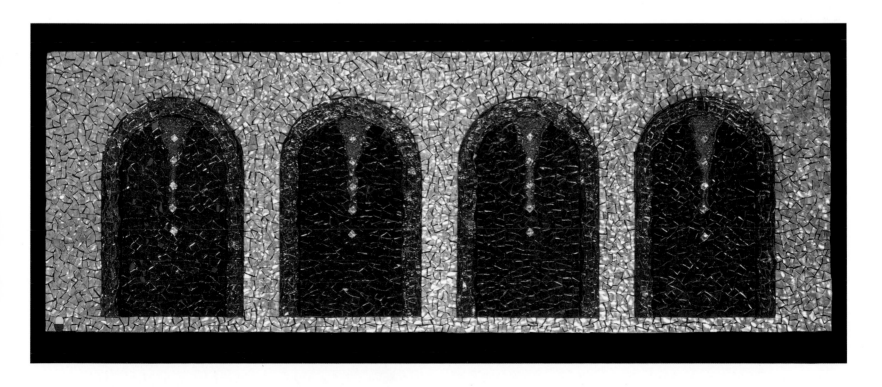

Renato Signorini (1908-1999). He then proceeded to show me around his impressive studios, which at that time were behind the basilica of San Vitale. It was a defining experience.

So, it was not the colors of the Byzantine mosaics but the light reflecting off the materials – smalti and gold – that was revealing. For the first time I was not looking – I was really seeing. I then pursued Byzantine-inspired mosaics. The light had allowed me – and anyone who looks – the ability to see the mosaics in a spirit of wonderment and receptive awareness.

In looking at Byzantine mosaics, there is no need for intellectual feedback – that is by acknowledging the stories of the religious subjects – only an insight into visual mysticism. It is this, I now know, that makes the greatest art, whether figurative or abstract.

With this knowledge in mind, my work evolved into an absolute abstraction, which may – or may not – be considered a means to mystic revelation. My only objectivity was to give a title to each specific work. Thus during the 1990s I explored my revelation, tentatively but with absolute conviction.

Through apperceiving the deepest meanings in each of my works it is my hope that mosaic, with its necessary harmonious placing of the tesserae, will help sensitize the eye and therefore the looking. Any enquiring mind in a search for or needing absolute truth may be able to pick up a pulsation of the rhythm that is life and therefore truth.

My aim through manipulating light in each mosaic is to crystallize a fragment of the beauty and order that lies beyond our sense of everyday knowing and intellectual explanation, and relay something of that pulse of original creation and our position in the wider world. I believe the Byzantine mosaic artists understood this when pictorializing their religious belief. I understand it from my unbelief.

As artists, our eyes are windows onto the realm beyond the comprehension of our senses, or if preferred, the soul. This understanding drives our compulsion to work – and mosaic is uniquely placed to explore this pursuit.

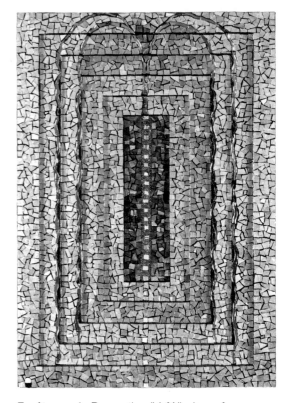

Fenêtre sur la Perception IV *(Window of Perception IV), by Elaine M Goodwin, 2006, 18in x 12in/46cm x 30cm, collection K. Taylor*

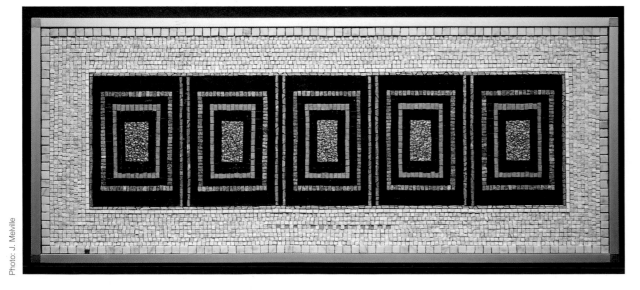

Photo: J. Melville

Metastasis, 1999,
*by Elaine M Goodwin,
62in x 22in / 158cm x 56cm*

## Method

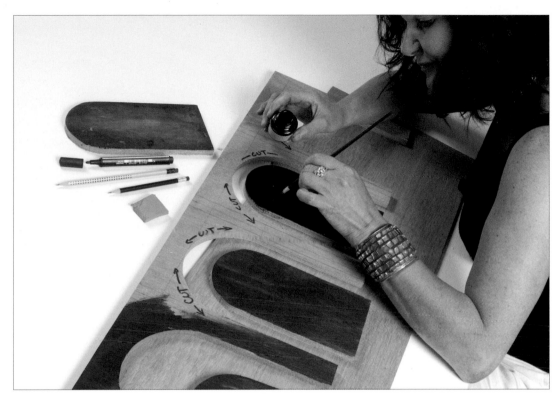

### The Drawing

Four identical arches with inner and outer lines were drawn onto the thicker plywood sheet and cut out, using an electric saw. The edges were smoothed with glass paper/sand paper.

### Equipment

¼in/ 6mm plywood (12in x 34in/30cm x 87cm),
½in/ 12 mm plywood (10¾in x 32in/18cm x 82cm),
    cut to shape with four equally-spaced
    rounded arch shapes
electric handsaw
sand/glass paper
pencil
ruler
black marker pen
wood adhesive
black ink
brushes
eraser

1 Painting the timber with black ink to give a dark setting surface. All the wooden surfaces were then brushed with a coat or two of black ink. This mosaic will not be grouted and any gaps will reflect this dark base, not the color of the timber. The black ground also acts as a good foil when cutting the silvery materials, as they show up clearly against such a dark ground. Glue the inner and outer shapes in position on the board.

### Materials

Ravenna mirror glass in a variety of silver shades
    and textures
Venetian white gold with plain and undulating
    surfaces
mosaic nippers
pva/white glue
container
black ink
brush
black sealer
palette knife
brush for dispersing glass shards

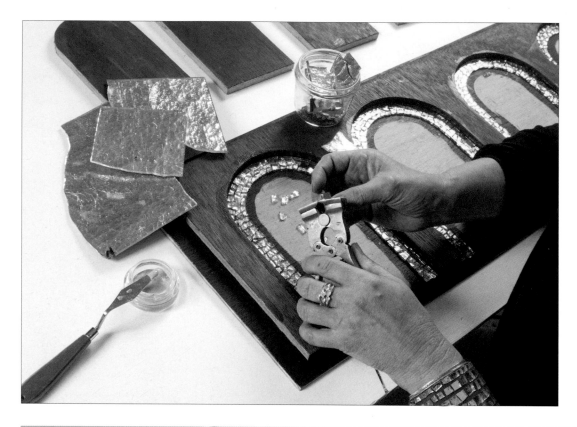

2 Cutting tesserae and building up the area between the arched shapes with silvered mirror glass. Begin work on the narrow arch-shaped band between the cut shapes, using a silver mirror glass in *opus palladianum*. Try to put the straightest edges on the outer and inner cut edges for a truer line. Cut a quantity of long undulating tesserae.

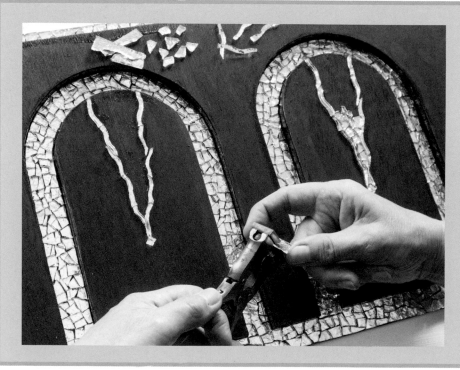

**Secret Insight 2**

Cutting narrow ribbons of undulating tesserae is not too difficult when you know the secret.

Undulating ribbons of glass or other materials can be accomplished by using extra pressure on the material to force a curved fracture.

Place the open edge of the nipper in the center of the tessera and then hold the tessera at the top and bottom edges. Gently add pressure from these edges at the same time as applying pressure to cut the tessera – eureka! – an undulating narrow ribbon of glass.

Use these wavy ribbons of tesserae to outline a V-shape within each raised arched section – an oblique reference to the early Byzantine bead curtains commonly seen in the mosaics of S. Appollinare in Classe in Ravenna, Italy, and in the Great Mosque of Damascus in Syria. Before fixing the tesserae, add a little permanent black coloring pigment or ink to the adhesive. Infill the area with mirror glass.

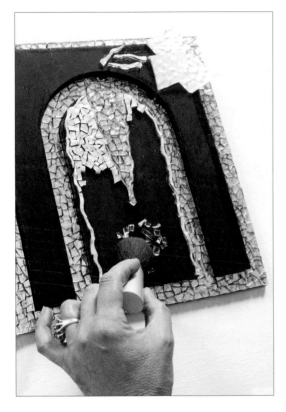

3 Cut further undulating tesserae in Venetian white gold to outline the raised arched area, and continue filling in this space with the same material. The varying heights of the material make up a gently shimmering opaque surface. The little brush is very necessary in clearing away small sharp shards of the cut glass, which always result when cutting tesserae.

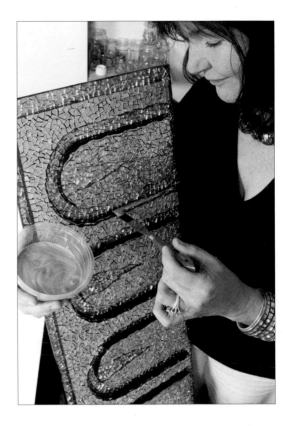

4 Filling in the background. The remaining background area is made up of Venetian white gold with a smooth surface. As the material is hand made, use the imperfections of height to greatest convenience, slightly angling the pieces with the adhesive individually applied on the back, onto the surrounding timber backing board.

5 When the piece is completed, seal the edges of the work with a proprietary black sealer. Put a little of the sealer in a container and using a palette knife carefully seal any exposed edge. This will protect the work, while the dark color also unifies the mosaic as a whole. Each of the four edges will be done in turn. When dry, clean the mosaic surface with cloths to remove any stray adhesive and fingerprints.

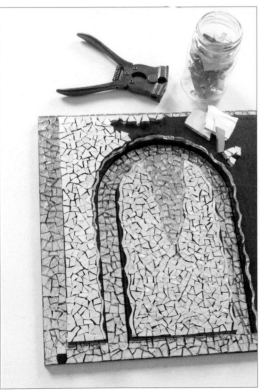

# Bibliography

Albertini, Bianca and Sandro Bagnoli, *Carlo Scarpa, Architecture in Details*, London, Architecture Design and Technology Press, Ltd., 1988.

Alexander, M. A., & M. Ennaifer, *Corpus des mosaïques de Tunisie*, Vol.1. *Utique*, Institut National d'Archéologie et d'Arts, Tunis, 1973.

Amanath, *Jaipur – the Last Destination*, New Delhi: India Bookhouse Pvt. Ltd., 1993.

Ashton, Dore, et al., *The Mosaics of Jeanne Reynal*, New York: October house Inc, 1969.

Avery, Catherine B., *Classical Handbook*, London: George Harrap & Co., 1962.

Bäumer, Angelica, *Gustav Klimt: Women*, London: Weidenfeld and Nicholson, 1986.

Borini, Giuseppe and Mario Pierpaoli, *Ravenna: Treasure of Light*, Ravenna: Longo Editore, 1991.

Cimok, Fatih, *Antioch Mosaics*, Turkey, A Turizm Yayinlari, 1995.

Clarke, John R., *Roman Black and White Figural Pavements*: New York: New York University Press, 1979.

Di Stefano, Carmela A., *Palermo Punica*, Palermo, Sicily: Museo Archeologico 'A. Salinas', 1995/96.

Farneti, Manuela, *Glossario tecnico-storico del mosaico*, Ravenna: Longo Editore, 1993.

Fiorentini Roncuzzi, Isotta, and Elisabeth Fiorentini, *Mosaic: Materials, Techniques and History*, Italy: MWcV Editions, 2002.

Fischer, Peter, *Mosaic: History and Techniques*, New York: McGraw Hill, 1971.

Fradier, Georges, *Mosaïques de Tunisie*, Tunis: Cérès Productions, 1976.

Fuks, Paul, *Picassiette: le Jardin d'Assiettes*, Neuchâtel: Idées et Calendes, 1992.

Giubelli, Giorgio, *Herculaneum*, Naples: Carcavallo editore, n.d.

Goldstone, Bud, and Ailoa Poquin Goldstone, *The Los Angeles Watta Towers*, London: Thames and Hudson, 1997.

Gouder, Tancred C., *The Mosaic Pavement in the Museum of Roman Antiquities*, Rabat, Malta: Department of Museums, 1983.

Grey, Michael, *Pre-Columbian Art*, London: Thames and Hudson, 1978.

Guglielmi, Carla Faldi, *Tesori d'arte cristiana: 14 Roma, S.Prassede*, Bologna: Officine Grafiche, 1966.

Hatay Archaeological Museum, *Hatay Museum and Environs*, Ankara: Dönmez Ofset Basımevi, n.d.

Lechopier, Claude, *Une mosaïque à ciel ouvert, la maison bleue de Dives-sur-Mer*, Cabourg: Editions Cahiers du Temps, 2004.Cabourg: Editions Cahiers du Temps, 2004.

Ligtelijn, Vincent, and Rein Saariste, *Josep M Jujol*, Rotterdam: Uitgeverij, OIO, 1996.

Ling, Roger, *Ancient Mosaics*, London: British Museum, Press, 1998.

Maizels, John, *Raw Creation; Outsider Art and Beyond*, London: Phaidon, 1996.

Morhange, Angelina, *Boris Anrep*, London: The National Gallery, 1979.

Önal, Mehmet, *Belkis/Zeugma and its Mosaics*, Turkey: Sanko Holding, 2007.

Pajares-Ayuela, Paloma, *Cosmatesque Ornament*, London: Thames and Hudson, 2002.

Pean, Richard, *Punic Tunisia*, Ed. Regie 3 / AMVPPC, 2002.

Permanyer, Lluis, *Gaudi of Barcelona*, Barcelona: Ediciones Poligrafa SA, 1997.

Piccirillo, Michele, *The Mosaics of Jordan*, Amman: American Center of Oriental Research (ACOR), 1993.

Plantin, Yves, & Françoise Blondel, *Eugene Grasset*, Paris: Imprimerie Manchand, 1980.

Prévert, Jaques, *Selections from* Paroles, San Francisco: City Lights/Pocket Poets Series, 1964.

Reynolds, Simon, *A Companion to the Mosaics of St Paul's Cathedral*, Norwich: Michael Russel (Publishing) Ltd., 1994.

Saint Phalle, Niki, *Niki de Saint Phalle, Oeuvres des années 80*, Paris: Galerie de France-JGM Galerie, 1989.

Tammisto, Antero, *Birds in Mosaic*, Rome: Acta Instituti Romani Finlandiae, 1997.

Trollope, Edward, *Illustrations of Ancient Art*, London: George Bell, 1854.

Unger, Hans, *Practical Mosaics*, London: Studio Vista, 1965.

# Mosaic Associations

### AIMC
*Associazione Internazionale Mosaicisti Contemporanei / International Association of Contemporary Mosaicists*
The AIMC was established in 1980 in Ravenna, Italy, with the aim of bringing together contemporary artists working in mosaic as a fine art medium. Its membership covers 40 countries and includes artists, architects, mosaic schools, restorers, art galleries, companies producing mosaic materials and tools, students, art critics and supporters. As well as functioning as a research institute, it holds a biennial conference to discuss subjects of common interest to its members.
http://www.aimcinternational.com/

### BAMM
*British Association for Modern Mosaic*
Established in 1999 with the aim of promoting, encouraging and supporting excellence in contemporary mosaic art, and raising public awareness of modern mosaic art and of the artists creating it. It does this through exhibitions, publications, events and related educational activities. http://www.bamm.org.uk

### MAAJ
*Mosaic Association of Japan*
Founded in 1995 to promote and support mosaic artists and their work, and to raise public awareness of mosaic art. It also serves as a center of information concerning worldwide activities in the mosaic arts. http://www6.big.or.jp/~mosaicjp/

### MAANZ
*Mosaic Association of Australia and New Zealand*
Formed in March 2002 as Mos-Oz, the Association has now expanded to include New Zealand, with the aim of raising the profile of mosaic as an art form. MAANZ is about mosaic exhibitions and mosaic education, and has a strong community focus. http://www.maanz.org

### MAAC
*Mosaic Art Association of Canada*
Set up in 2005, MAAC's mission is to promote mosaic art and artists in Canada by enhancing public awareness of mosaic art and by cultivating a supportive network of mosaic artists and enthusiasts. http://www.mosaicartcanada.org/

### SAMA
*Society of American Mosaic Artists*
Founded in 1999, is a non-profit organization dedicated to educating, inspiring, and promoting excellence in mosaic art. To achieve this, SAMA organizes programs, events, and activities to encourage an exploration to the full potential of the art. http://www.americanmosaics.org/

# International Schools

There are numerous schools world wide, from the very small and local to the established and international, both private and public, which aim to teach and encourage mosaic making. Those below are directly or indirectly associated with this publication.

Studio del Mosaico, St Peter in the Vatican, 00120 Vatican City,Italy
email: mosaico.vaticano@fsp.va
Established 16th century. Director: Paolo di Buono.

Scuola Mosaicisti del Friuli, Via Corridoni 6,
33097 Spilimbergo (PN), Italy
tel 00 39 9427 2077
www.scuolamosaicistifriuli.it
www.mosaicschool.org
Established 1922. President: Alido Gerussi

Istituto Statale d'Arte per il Mosaico – Gino Severini
Via Pietro Alighieri no. 8, 48100 Ravenna, Italy
tel.: 00 39 0544-38310
fax: 00 39 0544-31152
www.racine.ra.it/isaseverini/
Established 1960s. Director: Anna Giargoni

Institute Artistique Antonin,Dekwaneh, Beirut, Lebanon
tel. 00 96 11 68 22 52
fax 00 96 11 68 60 14
email: souhailnem@hotmail.com
Established 2003/04. Director: Souheil Ghanemin

'Mosaico Oggi', Associazione Culturale Arte Scienza Spettacolo,Via San Girolamo Emiliani, 15, 00152 Roma, Italy
tel. 00 39 0686 908269
tel./fax: 00 39 0699 85236
http://web.tiscali.fernandatollemeto
Established 2007. President: Fernanda Tollemeto

# Stockists

The major stockists for materials used in this publication:

### UK
Reed Harris (main showroom), Riverside House, 27 Carnwath Road, London SW6 6JE
tel: 00 44 (0) 20 77 36 75 11
fax: 00 44 (0) 20 77 36 29 88
email: enquiries@reed-harris.co.uk
www.reedharris.co.uk
*Manufactured ceramic, glazed and vitreous mosaic tiles, marble, stone*

Edgar Udny and Co Ltd, 314 Balham High Road, London, SW17 7AA
tel. 00 44 (0)20 87 67 81 81
fax 00 44 (0)20 87 67 77
www.applegate.co.uk/indexes/counties/all-london.htm
*Smalti, Venetian gold leaf glass, vitreous glass, ceramic mosaic tiles.*

Fothergill Engineering Fabrics Ltd, PO Box 1, Summit, Littleborough, Lancashire OL15, 0LR
*Fiber netting*
00 44 (0) 1706 372 414
00 44 (0) 1706 376 422
sales@fothergill.co.uk
www.fothergill.co.uk

### Italy
Angelo Orsoni s.r.l, Cannaregio 1045,30121, Venice, Italy.
tel. 00 39-041-244 0002 / 3
fax 00 39-041-524 0736
www.orsoni.com          email: info@orsoni.com
*Smalti, Venetian gold leaf glass (oro), hammer (martellina), hardie (tagliolo)*

Anna Fietta, Via Argentario 5, 48100 Ravenna, Italy
tel. 00 39-0544-213 728
fax 00 39-0544-213 728
www.annafietta.it          email: finelli@annafietta.it
*Mirror glass (vetri specchiati), millefiori (murrine)*

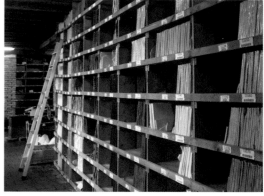
*Angelo Orsoni smalti "Library", detail, Cannaregio, Venice, Italy*

Photo: EMG

### France
Société Albertini et Cie,1 - 7 rue des Genêts, 95370, Montigny lès Cormeilles,France
tel: 00 33 (0) 1 39 97 25 80
fax: 00 33 (0) 1 34 50 69 59
*'Smalti' sheets (pâte de verre/émaux), glass materials*

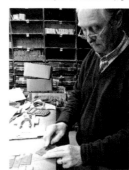
*Gérard Albertini cutting glass from his kilns, Paris, France*

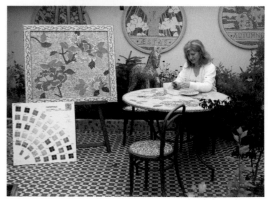
*Mosaic artist Nicole Depeu working with the enameled tiles of Briare, France*

Opiocolor Mosaiques, 4, Route de Cannes, 06650 OPIO, France
tel: 00 33 (0) 2 93 77 23 30
fax: 00 93 (0) 2 93 77 40 56
www.opiocolor.com
*Manufactured vitreous mosaic (pâte de verrre)*

Emaux de Briare (shop and museum of mosaic),
1 Boulevard Loreau, F-45250 Briare, France
tel.  00 33 (0)2 38 31 22 01
fax  00 33 (0)2 30 37 00 89
www.omauxrlebriare.com / musee.
email: mosaique@wanadoo.fr
*manufactured glazed, enameled and metallic surfaced tiles (émaux)*

**USA**
Mosaic Smalti
tel: 1-866-432-5369
www.mosaicsmalti.com
*US distributors for Angelo Orsoni glass and gold smalti*

di Mosaico
tel: 866-437-1985
www.dimosaico.com
*US distributor for Mosaici Donà Murano glass and gold smalti, and stone mosaic tiles*

Mosaic Art Supply
inspire@mosaicartsupply.com
www.mosaicartsupply.com
*Distributors of glass, marble, pebbles and tools*

Mosaic Mercantile
tel: 877-9-MOSAIC
www.mosaicmercantile.com
*Distributors of Italian glass and ceramic tile, pebbles, tools, grouts and adhesives*

**Canada**
Mosaic Art Source
info@mosaicartsource.com
www.mosaicartsource.com
*Distributors of glass tile, smalti, gold, millefiori and tools*

**Other countries**
Internet searches will reveal many other suppliers of mosaic materials and tools world-wide

# Index

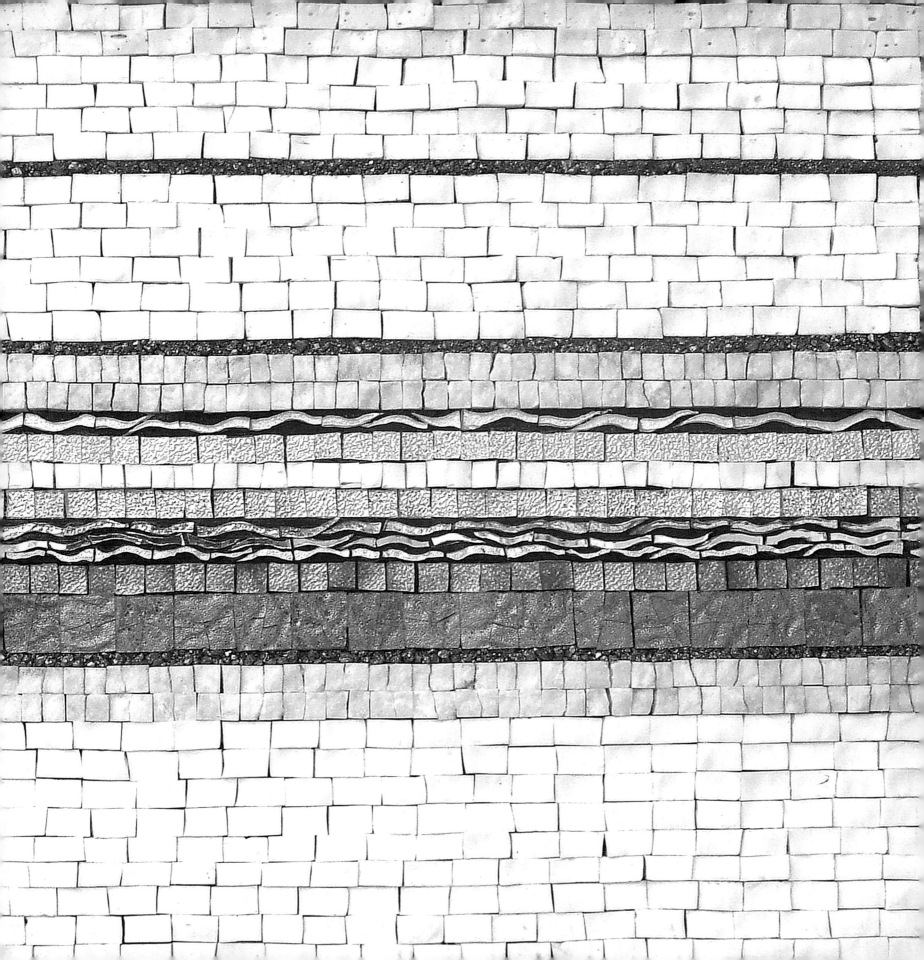